# Dazzling Secrets

## For

# Despondent Saints!

### Ken Chant

# Dazzling Secrets
# For Despondent Saints!

## Ken Chant

Revised 2012

ISBN 978 1-61529-067-3
Copyright © Ken Chant

Vision Publishing
1672 Main Street E 109
Ramona, CA 92065
1 800-9-VISION
www.booksbyvision.com

## A NOTE ON GENDER

It is unfortunate that the English language does not contain an adequate generic pronoun (especially in the singular number) that includes without bias both male and female. So *"he, him, his, man, mankind,"* with their plurals, must do the work for both sexes. Accordingly, wherever it is appropriate to do so in the following pages, please include the feminine gender in the masculine, and vice versa.

## FOOTNOTES

A work once fully referenced will thereafter be noted either by "ibid" or "op. cit."

# CONTENTS

# ABBREVIATIONS

Abbreviations commonly used for the books of the Bible are

| | | | |
|---|---|---|---|
| Genesis | Ge | Habakkuk | Hb |
| Exodus | Ex | Zephaniah | Zp |
| Leviticus | Le | Haggai | Hg |
| Numbers | Nu | Zechariah | Zc |
| Deuteronomy | De | Malachi | Mal |
| Joshua | Js | | |
| Judges | Jg | | |
| Ruth | Ru | Matthew | Mt |
| 1 Samuel | 1 Sa | Mark | Mk |
| 2 Samuel | 2 Sa | Luke | Lu |
| 1 Kings | 1 Kg | John | Jn |
| 2 Kings | 2 Kg | Acts | Ac |
| 1 Chronicles | 1 Ch | Romans | Ro |
| 2 Chronicles | 2 Ch | 1 Corinthians | 1 Co |
| Ezra | Ezr | 2 Corinthians | 2 Co |
| Nehemiah | Ne | Galatians | Ga |
| Esther | Es | Ephesians | Ep |
| Job | Jb | Philippians | Ph |
| Psalm | Ps | Colossians | Cl |
| Proverbs | Pr | 1 Thessalonians | 1 Th |
| Ecclesiastes | Ec | 2 Thessalonians | 2 Th |
| Song of Songs | Ca * | 1 Timothy | 1 Ti |
| Isaiah | Is | 2 Timothy | 2 Ti |
| Jeremiah | Je | Titus | Tit |
| Lamentations | La | Philemon | Phm |
| Ezekiel | Ez | Hebrews | He |
| Daniel | Da | James | Ja |
| Hosea | Ho | 1 Peter | 1 Pe |
| Joel | Jl | 2 Peter | 2 Pe |
| Amos | Am | 1 John | 1 Jn |
| Obadiah | Ob | 2 John | 2 Jn |
| Jonah | Jo | 3 John | 3 Jn |
| Micah | Mi | Jude | Ju |
| Nahum | Na | Revelation | Re |

*Ca* is an abbreviation of *Canticles*, a derivative of the Latin name of the *Song of Solomon*, which is sometimes also called the *Song of Songs*.

# DIAGNOSIS

*Every morning when you wake up you will groan,
"Oh, if only it were evening!" and in the evening
you will cry, "Oh, if only it were morning!" (De
28:66-67)*

Does that describe *you*, or perhaps someone you know? Recent
surveys suggest that 1 in 6 people will suffer a major depression in
their lifetime. Fifty years ago the average age of people suffering
from depression was 40; now it has fallen to the mid-20s. Among
teen-agers, suicide is one of the most common causes of death; in
some areas, it is the second most common cause.

What is the best remedy for depression? How can Christians
maintain a life of continual victory? These pages will present some
key ideas that can lift people out of the gloomy pit and keep them
living in the sunshine of God's love. You may not need help for
yourself; yet there are probably people around you who *are*
hurting. With these keys in your hand, you may be able to help
them escape from darkness and come into light.

You may notice the absence of any section in this book dealing
with the devil. That is not because I do not recognise his power to
destroy human life. I understand full well that he comes, as Jesus
said, only *"to steal, kill, and destroy"* (Jn 10:10). But despite
common opinion, Satan is seldom the immediate cause of
depression, and I felt he could be safely left out of these pages
(apart from an occasional reference here and there.)

If you want to know more about the devil and demons, you should
obtain my book on the subject, *Demonology*. [1] But here I am

---

[1] Demonology is a *VCC* text book. It contains a comprehensive study of the
kingdom of darkness, and is a permanent part of the *VCC* syllabus.

content to say only this much: the devil certainly does *"go around seeking whom he may devour"* (1 Pe 5:8-9), so we do need to take him into account. He may not often be the *instigator* of melancholy, but he and his minions do often try to take *advantage* of a gloomy state that already exists. Our duty, knowing that Satan can and does attack the saints (Re 13:7), is to resist him steadfastly in faith (Ja 4:7-8), confident of the victory that we have in Christ.

In his essay on the art of poetry Horace once said, "It is difficult to express ordinary ideas in a unique manner." Yet that is what I have tried to achieve in these pages. You will no doubt make your own judgment about whether or not I have succeeded. I certainly hope at least that you will discover here (even if "few and far between") some "subtle spells" akin to those described by Henry Kendall [2] in a lovely sonnet. He too had abandoned hope of perfection, and of complete originality. He was content in his latter years (as I am myself) to draw upon universal knowledge, and only occasionally to come delightedly upon scenes of wondrous beauty, which no other eye had before seen –

> I proposed once to take my pen and write,
> Not songs, like some, tormented and awry
> With passion, but a cunning harmony
> Of words and music caught from glen and height,
> And lucid colours born of woodland light
> And shining places where the sea-streams lie.
> But this was when the heat of youth glowed white,
> And since, I've put the faded purpose by.
> I have no faultless fruits to offer you
> Who read this book; but certain syllables

---

[2] Henry Kendall (1839-82) was an Australian poet, noted for lyrical poems about the bush and country life. He also wrote a number of fine narrative poems, which encompassed biblical and classical as well as Australian themes.

Herein are borrowed from unfooted dells
And secret hollows dear to noontide dew;
And these at least, though far between and few,
May catch the sense like subtle forest spells.

## CHAPTER ONE:

# NATURAL AND PHYSICAL

We can be too pious for our own good. We attribute bad days to some mysterious spiritual force, when the cause may be nothing more than a normal swing in the cycle of life. The devil is often blamed for problems his hand never touched!

We need to take account of these natural fluctuations. They reflect the way God has chosen to build a world in which everything moves around changing seasons. Tides rise and fall, winds surge and flow, the moon waxes and wanes, the whole earth is marked by a constant ebb and flow.

Inevitably, we ourselves experience the same shifts in our own daily affairs. Sometimes the "tide" is in, and sometimes it is out – but it will come back again. There are no mountains without valleys, and no valleys without mountains; if day is followed by night, just as surely night is followed by day. So the first rule in coping with depression is this –

## TAKE ACCOUNT OF NATURAL CYCLES

All professional athletes, performers, entertainers and public speakers experience good days and bad days – that is, times when it seems they can do nothing wrong, and other times when, no matter how hard they try, they can do nothing right! Christians are subject to the same fluctuations, although they often search unwisely for some deeper reason for a bad day.

A preacher, for example, may step out of the pulpit complaining that the devil put a blanket of ineptitude over his entire sermon. In reality, the fault was probably nothing more than a natural ebb in his usual skill. Or, the same man, if he has preached brilliantly, at once claims a special infusion of supernatural grace. More likely, he was just enjoying a good day! To attribute such variations to some profound spiritual cause is probably wrong. Most times the reason will be nothing more than an ordinary turning of the tide of life in one direction or another.

## CRICKET PLAYERS AND OTHERS

Sir Donald Bradman is reckoned by some to have been the most gifted athlete of all time. On a chart grading the performance of a cluster of brilliant sportsmen and women, he stands astonishingly far above the next highest. [3] Yet on the only occasion I went to a cricket ground to see Bradman bat in person, he failed. The world's greatest batsman walked out to the wicket, was clean-bowled by the first ball he faced, and walked back again to the pavilion!

If you prefer a baseball metaphor, we could say that even the very best players strike-out sometimes! Or think about tennis: today a player hits every ball right in the centre of his racquet and places each shot perfectly; but tomorrow he may hardly be able to get near the ball!

Occasionally I am able to attend a symphony concert, and while my hope of a pleasant evening listening to fine music is seldom disappointed, it is sometimes wonderfully exceeded. How? Because occasionally a strange magic happens in a concert hall. By some mysterious process, the maestro, the orchestra, the music, the audience, find themselves caught up in a marvellous harmony. The music rises from the mundane to the heavenly, and a performance

---

[3] A statistical survey of a number of top athletes and sportsmen shows that their performances can be averaged to give a common achievement of 29.1. A further calculation provides what is called a "standard deviation" of 13.3. When the same analysis is applied to Bradman, his "average is above the mean of 29.1 by more than five times the standard deviation. Statistical theory shows that the chance of something occurring so far from the mean is about one in a million." For that reason, the article in which I found these figures is titled, "Bradman – One in a Million!" It claims that we will have to wait 100,000 years before another athletic genius like Bradman appears!

that would have been merely competent is suddenly transformed into a supernal experience. If you were sitting there watching me, you would see tears of rapture shining in my eyes. On those nights, my soul is alive with a special joy, worship vibrates in my spirit, and paeons of praise to the Giver of divine music pour out of a grateful heart.

## A BAFFLING MYSTERY

Yet here is the strange thing: the same orchestra, playing the same music, to the same audience, a day later may lapse into a merely entertaining performance. What caused the magic in the earlier concert? Why did it vanish? No one knows. It seems weird, but seldom can any player or performer safely predict either success or failure. There is no way to determine whether on a particular day one will behave superbly or abysmally.

Sir Laurence Olivier was reckoned to be the greatest male Shakespearian actor of the 20th century, if not of all time. His dramatic powers were just as extraordinary on the screen as they were in the live theatre, so he was accustomed to receiving constant acclaim. But on one occasion, his performance reached such sensational heights that when he left the stage a thunderous standing ovation shook the building. However, as his fellow actors and the theatre staff later crowded around him, pouring out their congratulations, he was curt and angry. He swore at them, pushed his way through, and rushed distraught into the dressing room. His friends were bewildered. One of them finally approached the actor and asked, "Why are you so upset? Don't you know that your performance was marvellous?" Olivier replied with despair, "Of course I know! But I don't know how or why I was able to do it. So how do I know if I can ever do it again?"

## IT HAPPENS TO US TOO

We Christians, whether preachers or lay people, need to accept this fact: life runs in cycles; its tides rise and fall. We are not different from our neighbours. We too enjoy those wonderful days when it seems impossible to make a mistake, when everything around us works just as it should. Yet for no discernible reason we also experience those other dismal days, when everything goes wrong, when every effort fails and it feels like the whole world is against us.

Those who are wise recognise that no one can escape these ups and downs in the flow of life. Expecting good fortune to come and go, they will not be too much swayed by either a marvellous performance nor a poor one. They will be like Alfred the Great, who was king of Wessex in the 10th century. Sir Winston Churchill describes his calm approach to the inescapable vicissitudes of life –

> *(His) sublime power to rise above the whole force of*
> *circumstances, to remain unbiased by the extremes*
> *of victory or defeat, to persevere in the teeth of*
> *disaster, to greet returning fortune with a cool eye,*
> *to have faith in men after repeated betrayals, raises*
> *Alfred far above the turmoil of barbaric wars to his*
> *pinnacle of deathless glory.* [4]

What a striking phrase: he greeted "returning fortune with a cool eye"! Good news did not elate him unduly, nor did bad news crush him. He accepted that a defeat today could be turned into a victory tomorrow; but just as surely, today's triumph might become tomorrow's tragedy. Who knows what a day will bring? (Ja 4:13-15; Ec 7:14-16).

Similar wisdom was expressed by the Chinese philosopher Lao Tse, in his book *Tao-teh-King* –

> *(It is the way of Tao) not to act from any personal*
> *motive; to conduct affairs without feeling the*
> *trouble of them; to taste without being aware of the*

---

[4]    History of the English-Speaking Peoples, Vol 1, Ch 7.

*flavour; to account the great as small and the small
as great; to recompense injury with kindness.* [(5)]

One way to minimise the effect of these natural fluctuations, to smooth life's path, and to maintain good health and high vitality is to

## OBSERVE PROPER DIET AND REST

Never forget that God's healing covenant with Israel included obedience to a long list of laws about diet, hygiene, adequate rest, good work practices, proper relationships, and the like. People who chose to live foolishly, or to ignore God's rules, said Moses, could expect to reap a harvest of poor health and clouded prosperity (see De 28:58 ff.).

Those principles have not changed. A change of life-style is all that many people need to shift from gloom to gladness.

I plan now to advance to what some would call more "spiritual" keys to overcoming depression. Yet what could be more truly "spiritual" than to live sensibly, following the rule of *"moderation in all things"*? (Ph 4:5). Another rule states, *"the natural comes first, then the spiritual"* (1 Co 15:46).

However, after taking into account the normal rounds of life, and giving wise attention to diet, exercise, rest, and the like, some people can still find themselves mired in a swamp of despondency. So let us look at some other causes of melancholy, and their cure.

---

[(5)]   Quoted by Milton S. Terry, <u>Introduction to Homiletics</u>; Academia Books, Grand Rapids, undated; pg. 47.

## POINTS TO PONDER

➢ Do you agree with the assertion that Satan is seldom the immediate cause of mental or spiritual depression?

➢ Ponder those good and bad days when success or failure was mostly dependent upon quite ordinary natural factors.

➢ What does the anecdote about Sir Laurence Olivier tell us about the difficulty, if not impossibility, of changing the normal fluctuations of life?

➢ What did Sir Winston Churchill mean when he said that King Alfred the Great had a "cool eye"?

➢ Are you prone to experience, without an adequate cause, too many gloomy days? Perhaps you need to question your life-style – diet, work habits, rest, recreation, and the like.

*CHAPTER TWO:*

# OBEYING GOD

Why are people, especially Christians, so silly as to think they can defy God and get away with it? At the very least they should realise that the Lord will turn a deaf ear to their prayers –

> *If I nurture evil deeds in my heart, the Lord will not
> listen to me (Ps 66:18).*

No wonder they are depressed! How can anyone hope to be joyously alive if he or she knows, deep inside, that God will take no notice of them? Surely a sense of being isolated from God is enough to throw even a saint into the dismals.

So something has to be done about this problem of sin.

But what do we mean by *"sin"*?

Let me answer that by suggesting that sin can take two major forms –

## POSITIVE ACTION

By this I mean, deliberate action against God's command, doing something that you know God has forbidden. You might say, "But I can't help it!" Perhaps, but remember that people seldom do things they don't want to do. If you do wrong it is because you like the wrong you are doing, otherwise you wouldn't do it. How do I know? Just ask yourself how many sins you do _not_ commit? All the bad things you *could* do, but don't, because you don't like them! But this idea was expressed better by an old rabbi who lived some two centuries before Christ –

> *The Lord is indeed compassionate and full of mercy,
> always ready to forgive sin and to rescue those who
> are in trouble. But woe to those who have lost their
> nerve and given way to fear. Woe to hypocrites who*

*lead a double life. Woe to faint-hearts who have thrown away their faith – how will they be kept safe? Woe to those who have given up the struggle. What will you do when you have to meet God?*

*How dare you say, "It is the Lord's fault that I went astray!" It is your duty to avoid what God hates. How dare you say, "God himself led me into wrongdoing!" What use can God have for a sinner? . . . If you choose to do so, you can do what God wants; you can live faithfully, if you set your mind to it. . . . Yet God always leaves a door open for those who are sorry, to come back to him. So return to the Lord, and be done with sin, and learn how to hate what he hates. . . . The Lord's mercy toward those who turn to him and renounce all sin is too great to measure!" (Sirach 2:10-14; 15:11-17; 17:14, 24-29.)*

## TRUE EMPIRE-BUILDERS

One of the handsome young knights in the brilliant court of King Henry VIII was Sir Thomas Wyatt. He served the monarch well and gained many honours, but he is remembered today chiefly for his poetry. In one of his odes he comments on the need for self-control, and echoes *Proverbs,* which insists that someone who can rule his own spirit is mightier than someone who merely conquers a city (16:32) –

> If thou wilt mighty be, flee from the rage
> Of cruel will; and see thou keep thee free
> From the foul yoke of sensual bondage:
> For though thine empire stretch to Indian sea,
> And for thy fear trembleth the farthest Thule,

If thy desire have over thee the power,
Subject then art thou, and no governor. [6]

Make your choice: will you be a subject or a governor? A slave or a ruler? If you choose freedom, it is yours in Christ. *"Turn to the Lord,"* cries Paul, *"and you will be changed into his likeness from glory to glory; for where the Spirit of the Lord is, there is perfect liberty!"* (2 Co 3:16-18). What the blood of Christ washes away, the Spirit of Christ will give you strength to overcome. We are called and enabled to be *"more than conquerors"* (Ro 8:37). Why would you settle for less? So turn your back on all that displeases the Father, and determine that you *will* be a good, true, and faithful Christian. There is no other pathway to true happiness.

## NEGATIVE ACTION

"Sin" is more than disobeying God, it may also result from ignoring God's command. It can be just as much an act of *omission* as of *commission*. Remember that Jesus did not merely *hate iniquity*, he also *loved righteousness* (He 1:9). Just as important as learning what God disapproves is learning what he approves, and wanting with all your heart what he wants.

Do you really want what God wants? Very few people do. Most of us want some part of the Lord's promised blessing, but seldom do we crave *everything* that lies in the divine purpose. We want the Lord to be involved in our lives, yet there usually remain a few corners we prefer him to stay out of. We hope that God will be close to us, but not too close.

That is why sometimes we do not get our prayers answered. It tends to be all or nothing with God. If we do not want the whole blessing we may not get any.

---

[6]   Songs #24, stanza one.

Our problem is that the Lord usually wants to bring us into a far more radical change than we are willing to accept.

For example, there are sick people who ask for healing, yet are not made well. Why?

Sometimes it is because at heart they do not want a miracle. They ask for prayer only because they feel they should, or because their sickness has become too troublesome. But they would be very unhappy if the Lord did anything more than relieve the worst of their symptoms. Their sickness brings them too many advantages. Perhaps it allows them to escape from responsibility; or they like being the centre of everyone's attention, fussed over and cared for each day.

Sometimes, too, people use sickness as an excuse for some other weakness that they lack the courage to deal with. So although they go through the motions of asking the Lord to make them fully well, they are actually hoping he will do no more than make them a little more comfortable in their sickness.

Yet Jesus was emphatic. He has scant patience with lukewarmness, with people who are content to get only a part of what God wants for their lives (Re 3:15-16). What joy can they expect? How can God be pleased with them? How long will he tolerate such pusillanimity? They should not be surprised when a pall of gloom enshrouds them.

Who will be filled with an abounding measure of the goodness and joy of the Lord? Only those who *"hunger and thirst"* for the blessing of God with all their heart! (Lu 6:21)

## PERFECT FREEDOM

Here then is an essential key to overcoming depression: yield to Christ your total and obedient service. You will find, not chains but liberty; not sorrow but joy; not death but life.

There is no substitute for obedience, there is no other pathway to joy, nor any other way to escape the depredations of the enemy –

*O God, who art the author of peace and lover of concord, in knowledge of whom standeth our eternal life, **whose service is perfect freedom**, defend us thy humble servants in all assaults of our enemies.* [7]

---

[7] From the Anglican <u>Prayer Book</u> of 1662; Second Collect: for Peace.

**POINTS TO PONDER**

➢ The most obvious cause of unanswered prayer is sin. We all need to examine ourselves from time to time on this matter (1 Co 11:27-30).

➢ Meditate on Sir Thomas Wyatt's *Ode*, especially his claim that the monarch of a vast empire is no better than a slave if he cannot rule himself.

➢ How true is this: sin is found more in what we fail to do than in what we do?

➢ What level of victory has God appointed for us in Christ? Little or much? How far have you gone toward reaching the Father's purpose?

➢ Not every person who asks God for a miracle of healing really wants it. Why not?

➢ What does Christ say about half-hearted faith, and what level of commitment does he demand from his disciples?

## CHAPTER THREE:

# BREAK THE GRIP OF SHAME

In the year 1400 King Richard II was foully murdered in Pontefract castle. It was a sorry end to a reign that had begun well. Under the king's beneficent and enlightened rule, *Merrie England* well deserved her name, and the realm prospered joyfully. But then Richard came increasingly under the sway of a group of unscrupulous advisors, who together brought the nation to a chaos of rapine and ruin. The king's cousin Henry Bolingbroke fomented a successful rebellion against him and seized the throne. Richard was imprisoned by Henry, who probably also instigated his death by starvation.

Shakespeare tells the unhappy story of Richard II in his play of the same name. One of the most dramatic scenes occurs when John of Gaunt (the Duke of Lancaster, the king's uncle) gives a speech some twelve months before the king's death, and laments the miseries that have fallen upon the land –

> This royal throne of kings, this scept'red isle,
> This earth of majesty, this seat of Mars,
> This other Eden, demi-paradise,
> This fortress built by Nature for herself
> Against infection and the hand of war,
> This happy breed of men, this little world,
> This precious stone set in the silver sea,
> Which serves it in the office of a wall,
> Or as a moat defensive to a house,
> Against the envy of less happier lands;
> This blessed plot, this earth, this realm, this England,
> This nurse, this teeming womb of royal kings . . .
> England, bound in with the triumphant sea,
> Whose rocky shore beats back the envious siege
> Of wat'ry Neptune, is now ***bound in with shame*** . . .

Just as England should have been a happy and blessed land, basking in the favour of God, but instead had become imprisoned by fetters of shame, so are many Christians today. They are guilty of a fault against which the writer of *Proverbs* long ago sounded a warning –

"Look straight ahead with honest confidence; **don't hang** your **head in shame**!" [8]

Here then is one of the commonest and most crippling problems facing the church – thousands of stumbling saints disabled by their shame. We talk today about being "shamefaced". But that modern word is actually a corruption of an older one, "shamefast" – that is, "held fast by shame" – which shows that our forefathers had a good sense of the crippling effect of improper shame. The sad thing is that many Christians who are indeed "held fast" in a prison of shame, need not be. They could, and they should be able to heed God's command, *"Don't hang your head in shame, but look straight ahead with honest confidence!"* Notice too, it *is* a command, which we should be as willing to obey as any other in scripture. How can we do this?

## WHAT DOES "SHAME" MEAN?

Observe first that there are two kinds of shame, one *good*, the other *bad*. Sirach spoke about it long ago (c. 180 BC) –

> ➢ Some people are too modest for their own good. They go beyond the true humility that every good person approves, and cling instead to a distorted shame that is actually sinful (4:20-21).

Notice also how "shame" differs from "guilt". We Christians know how to rid ourselves of *guilt* (by repentance and trust in the blood

[8] Pr 4:25 GNB, in a paraphrase that well captures the sense of the Hebrew idiom.

of Jesus); but often *shame* lingers on, stifling our best endeavours. That false shame, as our text demands, we must confront and cast aside, so that we can walk on confidently, with our heads held high!

Because of his vast experience and shrewd insight, the old rabbi [9] is a useful authority to consult on these matters. He had quite a bit to say about both kinds of shame –

## 1) THE RIGHT KIND OF SHAME

In a delightful passage (41:17-24) Sirach lists a number of things that any well-bred person would scorn, and among them he includes –

> sexual misconduct
> telling lies
> committing a crime
> disturbing the peace
> cheating a friend
> stealing anything from anybody
> scorning an offer of kindness
> ignoring a greeting
> repeating gossip
> telling someone else's secret
> giving cold-hearted charity
> ogling a lovely woman
> – and the like.

Sirach gave those instructions to the young men (*"my sons"* [10]) he was training to be rabbis. He also admonished them, *"Never put*

---

[9] Sirach is thought to have been about 80 years old when, after a lifetime of faithful, adventurous, and sometimes dangerous service (34:10-12), he wrote his *Book of Wisdom*.

[10] 2:1; 3:1; etc.

*your elbows on the table at meal-times!"* [11] Why such a
seemingly frivolous rule? It sounds incongruous, even ridiculous,
when put alongside a law against adultery. But Sirach was aiming
for a total lifestyle, one that was gracious, considerate, dignified,
pleasing to all. He was not merely making a list of prohibitions, but
creating a picture of a person who is well-mannered and courteous,
in matters both small and great. He was trying to build servants of
God whose behaviour would never bring a blush to anyone's
cheek. Gently spoken, discreet, upright, held back by a healthy
sense of shame from doing anything harmful, such people, says
Sirach, *"will be popular everywhere!"* (vs. 24). [12] They show a
*"proper shame"*, and will be commended by everyone.

So there is a positive sort of shame that we should all cultivate. It
keeps us from making fools of ourselves; it holds us back from
disgraceful, rude, or boorish behaviour; it makes us well-
mannered, it offends no one, it pleases God.

But then there is also

## 2) THE WRONG KIND OF SHAME

There is a negative destructive shame, which we must banish
before we can hope to live with true freedom and victory in Christ.
This is the shame condemned both in our text and by Sirach –

> *My son, with true humility maintain a proper
> estimation of your worth and hold to your self-
> respect. Who will admire you if you are ashamed of
> yourself; who will speak well of you if you
> disparage yourself? ... False shame may cost your
> very life; it will make you seem a fool in the eyes of*

---

[11] Your parents may have tried to teach you the same lesson, never knowing
where the rule came from. As you can see, it dates back at least 2200 years!

[12] In some translations, the reference is not 41:24 but 42:2.

*others. ... If you think I know what I am talking about, then you will accept that it is not good to go around always feeling ashamed; some self-abasement is good, but too much of it will destroy you! ... When you learn when to be ashamed and when not to be ashamed, then you will gain universal approval. (10:28-29; 20:22; 41:16; 42:1)*

Sirach knew that the young men he was training to be rabbis would bring only hurt to themselves and to others if they did not learn to overcome the tendency toward false shame that cripples so many earnest people. But why is this so? Surely shame is a virtue; surely it is a mark of true religion? Certainly, that is true of the right kind of shame. But this other kind is ruinous. Which brings us to the question –

## WHY IS THIS SHAME HARMFUL?

### 1) SHAME DESTROYS PERSONAL CONFIDENCE

False shame leads to a sense of incompetence, of unfitness for the task; it brings with it a gloomy apprehension of failure, or worse, an inbuilt tendency to cause one's own ruin out of a sense of getting one's just deserts. Indeed, people are seldom able either to receive or to hold what they feel they do not deserve. For example, both in the USA and in Australia I have read reports on how people are affected when they suddenly win a fortune in a lottery. An article in the Australian *Bulletin* (Aug 23rd, 1994) assessed the impact upon 21 lottery winners who became instant millionaires. Only two of them managed to put their winnings to good use. Among the remainder there were relationship break-ups, divorces, and a cluster of other human tragedies. One couple (who had previously been debt-free), before they had even collected their winnings, managed to spend the entire sum plus a further $20,000 – which they had borrowed!

People who cannot persuade themselves that they deserve to be rich, or whose new-found wealth plagues them with a sense of guilt or of unworthiness, will find some way – usually foolish – to rid themselves of the burden. They often add also some kind of active punishment, a self-imposed penalty for daring to hold even briefly what was not rightly theirs. Thus they plunge into debt; they spend the money stupidly; they commit a social outrage; they attack their loved ones, friends, and neighbours; they find ways to hurt, humiliate, or disgrace themselves.

The same problem often cripples Christian men and women. They cannot think themselves deserving any high favour from God. So they may fail altogether to expect any fulfilment of God's gracious promises; or, if the Father *should* happen to give them some superlative blessing, they swiftly find a way to destroy or nullify it. I have met pastors like that. Whenever a breath of revival begins to refresh their churches, whenever there is a surge of life and growth, they unknowingly set themselves to drive it away, and to crush the church back to its former meagre size and shape. A distorted sense of sin, a twisted feeling of unworthiness, has convinced them that they do not merit any signal favour from heaven.

So false shame prevents people either from *gaining* the promise of God, or from *keeping* it. Those who are wise will find such a state intolerable. they will rise up in Jesus' name and declare themselves fit in Christ, and by the blood of the covenant, to receive and to retain the highest and best of the Father's gifts.

## 2)  SHAME DESTROYS SOCIAL ASSURANCE

Where shame holds sway there will also be a feeling of insecurity. The *"shamefast"* feel threatened by life and society; they cannot believe that they merit the support and help of their neighbours.

In 1902 the British heavyweight boxing champion, R. P. Fitzsimmons, sailed to the USA for a challenge match against the American champion, J. J. Jeffries. When Mr Fitzsimmons arrived in San Francisco the newspaper reporters noticed that he was smaller than the American. They asked him if he was worried about the disparity in size. At once Fitzsimmons came back with the immortal rejoinder, "The heavier they are, the harder they fall!"

What supreme self-confidence! He had no shame of his shorter inches and lower poundage, but accepted himself as he was, and made the very best of it. It is a parable for us.

### 3)  SHAME DESTROYS SPIRITUAL AUTHORITY

How well the devil plays on this fault, striving to block all attempts to deal with the problem. Satan knows that if he can lock a believer into needless feelings of shame, then he will paralyse that believer's spiritual life. Effective witness and service for Christ will become a thing of the past.

How can anyone racked with shame pray with authority, or heal the sick, or cast out a demon, or move a mountain, or seize a miracle from God? Shame suffocates the soul. It chills faith; it deadens the spirit; it strangles worship; it turns someone who might have been a warrior for God into an emaciated weakling.

### 4)  SHAME DESTROYS HEAVENLY EXPECTATIONS

An ashamed believer dares not expect God to do anything great and wonderful. Such a trembling soul cries out, "Has not God's trust been betrayed? Have I not failed him dismally? Surely he is filled with fury? Oh, I know that the Lord has forgiven my sin; but how can a person so undeserving and unworthy as I, ever again hope for restoration to the highest benediction of heaven?"

But such cringing timorousness should have no place in Christian life. We are called to better things! Cast off this false shame! Be done with it! Strip it from your soul! Find a new place in the heavenlies in Christ! Which leads to our next question –

## HOW CAN SHAME BE OVERCOME?

The first and most necessary step is to recognise the problem – that step by itself will take you at least half of the way to victory!

But added to that you should also –

## 1) LOOK TO JESUS

During his astonishingly successful campaign against the Persian Empire, Alexander the Great once made his army take up winter quarters outside the walls of Babylon, where they remained for several months. Toward the end of winter, as the time drew near to renew the war, Alexander observed that his troops were sadly demoralised. He made enquiries, and discovered that most of his soldiers were heavily in debt to the Babylonian merchants and money-lenders. Nor had they any means to rid themselves of the burden. The men were therefore dispirited and fearful of punishment. They knew that their king was scrupulous in his dealings with those who had come into alliance with him, and would certainly punish debt defaulters.

Alexander realised that he had no alternative but to resolve the matter himself. So, although the soldiers' own extravagance was the cause of their misery, he announced that he himself would pay all their bills out of the royal treasury. But the men thought it was a trap to reveal the most culpable, who would then be condemned to severe exemplary discipline. No one dared to make his needs known.

Then Alexander, knowing that the troops were held back by shame and anxiety, ordered his officers to set up a line of tables, upon which was piled a vast number of golden coins, equalling 10,000 talents. The king assembled the army in front of the tables, stood up among the mounds of coins, and promised on his own honour, as their commander and sovereign, that any man who came would have his debt at once paid. At last the men gathered courage, took the king at his word, and began to come forward. That day, with no recriminations, every financial burden was lifted from the army, so that with renewed exhilaration they marched out to complete the rout of the Persians.

In the same way we Christians, who are the army of God, cannot hope to wage successful war against our spiritual foes if we are demoralised by shame, or stifled by an anxious fear of divine punishment. So Christ took our burden upon himself. He endured shame so that we could escape it - see Hebrews 12:2; and 1 Peter 2:6

The word "shame" comes from an Old English word that meant "to cover something over" – especially the naked body; [13] and still today shame is an attempt to paper over a sense of nakedness and vulnerability. But it cannot be done. We are helpless to ease the weight of our debt to God. So this false shame, which is really just an attempt to appease heaven's wrath by some pious act of our own, must be faced and cast aside. Let the blood of Jesus be your only and altogether sufficient covering.

## 2) LOOK TO THE PROMISE

What marvellous things are spoken of each believer in scripture! We are declared fully righteous in Christ, seated with him in heavenly places, made more than conquerors, blessed with every spiritual blessing, able to do all things, strengthened with divine might, pronounced his heirs, awarded an indescribably glorious destiny. But how hard it is for us to accept these affirmations! Our awareness of our own sin makes us more inclined to echo McBeth's lament –

> What hands are here? Ha, they pluck out mine eyes!
> Will all great Neptune's ocean wash this blood
> Clean from my hand? No, this my hand will rather
> The multitudinous seas incarnadine,
> Making the green one red.[14]

Like the sorrowing king, we too are inclined to fear that our sin, so black, so measureless, is surely enough to discolour the entire

---

[13] The word "chemise" - a kind of shirt - comes from the same root.

[14] The Tragedies; Volume One; *The Tragedy of McBeth*; Act 2, Scene 2; Shakespeare The Heritage Press; Norwalk Ct.

ocean of divine grace with its foulness. What folly (we think) to hope that such iniquity can be forgiven and forgotten in a moment!

Yet the gospel shouts that it is even greater folly to suppose that the sin of any person, or indeed of the whole of humanity, is enough to overwhelm the mercy the Father has gained for us in Christ. Take a bottle of red ink down to the beach. Pour the ink into the water. Will it dye the ocean crimson? Hardly! For a few moments a vivid stain will appear in the surrounding water, then the shifting waves will disperse the colour, absorb it, and cause it to vanish for ever. Can you stop a hurricane with a paper fan? Can you quench the sun with a pail of water? Can you brush the stars from the sky with a broom? You may do any of those things sooner than your sin can outreach the grace of God in Christ!

The challenge is upon us to believe God's promise heartily, and out of that faith to develop a positive self-image and joyful self-esteem, ridding ourselves of false shame. Once sin has been acknowledged, properly confessed to God and repented, and pardon claimed by the blood of the cross, then we stand sure in the promise that *"he is faithful and just, and will forgive our sin, and will cleanse us from all unrighteousness"* (1 Jn 1:9).

### 3) LOOK TO THE SPIRIT

What a boon we have in Holy Spirit baptism! Can we be so bad if the Holy Spirit is pleased to dwell in us? Are we not his holy Temples? (1 Co 3:16) This of course is no excuse to engage in sin; on the contrary, knowing that the Holy Spirit dwells within us should be the best incentive to shun wickedness and to pursue holiness avidly (vs. 17; 6:19-20; 2 Co 6:16-18).

But if you are baptised in the Holy Spirit, then rise up in the resident strength of that same Spirit. Allow him to fashion in you a new boldness, an innate confidence, a head held high. Let him take the dullness from your eye, the heaviness from your heart, the reluctance from your spirit, the shame from your soul!

# CONCLUSION

We all have many things to be ashamed of, in thought, word, and deed. No doubt you have sincerely repented of that past wrongdoing, and found the pardon and peace of God, his removal of all guilt. But have you handled the ongoing problem of shame? For some, release from that crippling manacle will come in a moment of prayer; others may need a longer time. But in any case, this day, right now, is the time to start! How should you walk this day? Only one way – as God's new creation in Christ Jesus "look straight ahead with honest confidence; **don't hang your head in shame**!"

## POINTS TO PONDER

➤ Is it possible to be too modest, or to be modest about the wrong things?

➤ What is the use of rules about good and bad table manners?

➤ Ponder the significance of the four ways in which false shame is harmful, and ask if these factors are applicable to yourself, or to someone you know.

➤ Do you understand why we need to apply the atoning death of Christ not only to sin but also to the crippling shame that can arise from sin?

➤ Locate some other biblical promises whose horizons, whose height and depth, reach far beyond the limits of human hurt and need.

➤ Contemplate the effect of the indwelling Spirit, both *negative* (warning against sin), and *positive* (affirming our security in Christ).

## CHAPTER FOUR:

# LACK OF VISION

We are a people of tomorrow. We have a destiny to fulfil, a prize to win, a kingdom to inherit.

This means that vibrant Christian life cannot be sustained by people who live within the confines of only one day. What Christian, whose horizon is bounded by the earth and its affairs, can hope to breathe the ethereal airs of heaven, or drink from the elysian fountain? As the wise man said, *"Without a vision, the people perish"* (Pr 29:18).

This lack of a future perspective takes us to the root cause of much depression. Surely the saddest people in the world must be Christians who have forgotten how to live on the edge of eternity, who have lost sight of the glorious City of God. We may all be in the gutter (as Lord Darlington said), but that should not prevent us from looking at the stars! [15]

But in the gutter or out of it, we Christians are marked by God as

## A PEOPLE OF DESTINY

What a marvellous destiny God has appointed for us in Christ! To live with a clear vision of the coming Kingdom of God is to live with excitement! Here is a dream that can add dramatic meaning to the most routine daily task. Even the meanest duty is transformed into another step on the stairway to Paradise!

---

[15] Oscar Wilde, Lady Windermere's Fan, Act III.

When such a magnificent prospect is so vividly set before us, I am constantly astonished by how many dull Christians I meet. Why are they not sparkling with vitality? An enquiry shows the reason: they have failed to *"see the King in all his splendour"* (Is 33:17-24); they lack any interest in the resplendent future God has appointed for us in Christ. No wonder they find life drab and their duty dreary.

To escape from that slough of despond we must –

## PRESS ON TOWARD THE GOAL

> *Dear friends, I cannot claim yet to have grasped all that God has for me in Christ, but this I can say: forgetting what lies behind me, and pressing forward to what lies ahead, I am straining toward the finishing line, so that I might win the prize of the high calling of God in Christ (Ph 3:13-14).*

Note that Paul had not yet arrived. He was still travelling toward the goal, still reaching for the best. No one in this life can truthfully claim to have apprehended everything that God has appointed for us in Christ. We all fall short in many things. But every right-thinking Christian should at least be marked by this: *they are pressing on!* We may stumble and fall from time to time, but we dare not lie there, wallowing in self-pity, mired in defeat. We must pick ourselves up, dust ourselves off, breathe the name of Jesus, *and go on again, unflagging in our determination to reach the goal and to gain the prize!*

This was the scene captured by John Bunyan in his allegory, *Pilgrim's Progress*. Christian had been set firmly on his pathway by Evangelist, who wished to encourage him still further, so he said to the pilgrim –

> *Do you see yonder shining light? (Christian) said, I think I do. Then said Evangelist, Keep that light in your eye, and go up directly thereto . . . So I saw in my dream that the man began to run. . .*

*(Christian travelled some distance on his journey, accompanied by another pilgrim, Hopeful, all the time keeping his eye fixed on that heavenly glow. Later they met some Shepherds, who conducted them to the top of a high hill.)*

*By this time the pilgrims had a desire to go forward, and the Shepherds a desire that they should; so they walked together toward the end of the mountains.*

*Then said the Shepherds one to another, Let us here show the pilgrims the gates of the Celestial City, if they have the skill to look through our perspective-glass. The pilgrims then lovingly accepted the motion: so they had them to the top of a high hill called Clear, and gave them the glass to look . . . (and) they thought they saw something like the gate, and also some of the glory of the place."*

*(Encouraged by that vision the pilgrims wended their way down the mountain, into the valley below, and continued bravely on their journey.)*[16]

We too need to learn how to step back from the daily task and see the vision of what God has in store for us. That image can change a dreary day into one thrilled by glad anticipation! (Ro 8:18).

However, we can capture this dazzling dream of God only if we –

## LIVE FOR ETERNAL VALUES

It is difficult to be kind to the folly of people whose boundaries never extend beyond the present hour, who build treasures on earth, but remain poor in heaven! Have they never read about the

---

[16] Pilgrim's Progress; John Bunyan 1678

only riches that cannot turn to dust, those that are found in the kingdom of God? Have they never heard the Spirit whisper in their souls, *"Set your affections on things above, not on those below."* (Cl 3:1-3). Are they so dull of eye and heavy of ear that the sight of heaven's beauty and the sound of heaven's melody must always elude them? Have they never learned the fine art of *"seeing the invisible"*? (1 Co 4:18). Why do they treat the visible world as if it is indestructible, when it is actually as transient as a cloud, as ephemeral as a leaf, destined to be rolled up and thrown away like an old rag? (He 1:10-12).

## THE WEIGHT OF GLORY

Is your outer nature wearing away? It can become inwardly renewed! Do your troubles seem many and burdensome? They can become light and insignificant! But only when you have captured the *feel* of what God is preparing for his church: *"an eternal weight of immeasurable glory."* To see that lustrous vision, to sense the weight of that grandeur, says Paul, causes everything in this world to shrink almost to nothing! (1 Co 4:16-18; Ro 8:18). So if you have lost heart, this is the way to regain your zest!

Robert Browning, in his poem *Cleon,* describes a sorrowful king, Protus, who voices two laments: he complains that when he is dead nothing of his sovereign glory will remain; and he thinks it is unfair that his friend, a poet and artist named Cleon, will live on in his deathless art. Let me take up the story at the point where Cleon the poet is addressing King Protus –

> "Thou askest if (my soul in men's hearts)
> I must not be accounted to attain
> The very crown and proper end of life.
> Enquiring thence how, now life closeth up,
> I face death with success in my right hand:
> Whether I fear death less than dost thyself
> The fortunate of men. "For" (writest thou)
> "Thou leavest much behind, while I leave nought:
> Thy life stays in the poems men shall sing,

The pictures men shall study; while my life,
Complete and whole now in its power and joy,
Dies altogether with my brain and arm,
Is lost indeed; since, – what survives myself?
The brazen statue that o'erlooks my grave,
Set on the promontory which I named.
And that – some supple courtier of my heir
Shall use its robed and sceptred arm, perhaps,
To fix the rope to, which best drags it down . . ."[17]

King Protus could hope to leave nothing more of himself than a statue, which he well knew some later monarch would pull down and replace with his own effigy. He had discovered too late a lesson we must all learn: the only lasting edifice is one built by "fixing our souls in men's hearts". There is no better "crown and proper end of life" than this: to write your name in the character other people, giving them a new song to sing, a new beauty to live by, a new hope to die for. So the king, who had once thought himself "the most fortunate of men", now realised that he was unfortunate; while the poet, whom the king had once deemed nothing, was now seen to have gained an undying renown.

By the grace of God, we Christians can achieve that goal better than any poet or artist. Can we not impart to those around us the love of Christ and the joy of heaven? And having done that, our life on earth gains undying value, and our eternal renown is secure!

## PREPARE FOR DEATH

Since we must all die, what can be more inane than failure to prepare for it? Thomas Carlyle tells a story about King Louis XV of France –

---

[17] Browning's Dramatic Monologues; Robert Browning; *Cleon;* The Folio Society, 1991

*Louis XV had always the kingliest abhorrence of Death. . . . He would not suffer Death to be spoken of; avoided the sight of churchyards, funereal monuments, and whatsoever could bring it to mind. It is the resource of the Ostrich; who, hard-hunted, sticks his foolish head in the ground, and would fain forget that his foolish unseeing body is not unseen too. . . .*

*We can figure the thoughts of Louis that day, when, all royally caparisoned for hunting, he met, at some sudden turning in the Wood of Senart, a ragged Peasant with a coffin: "For whom?" It was for a poor brother slave, whom Majesty had sometimes noticed slaving in those quarters. "What did he die of?" – "Of hunger:" – the King gave his steed the spur.*

*But figure his thought, when Death is now clutching at his own heart-strings; unlooked for; inexorable! Yes, poor Louis, Death has found thee. . . . Time is done, and all the scaffolding of Time falls wrecked with hideous clangour around thy soul: the pale Kingdoms yawn open; there thou must enter, all un-king'd, and await what is appointed thee! .*

*And yet let no meanest man lay flattering unction to his soul. Louis was a Ruler; but art not thou also one? His wide France, look at it from the Fixed Stars (themselves not yet Infinitude), is no wider than thy narrow brickfield, where thou too didst faithfully, or didst unfaithfully. Man, "Symbol of Eternity imprisoned into Time!" it is not thy works, which are all mortal, infinitely little, and the greatest no greater than the least, but only the Spirit thou workest in, that can have worth or continuance.* [18]

Louis ruled fair France; but we too, said Carlyle, have our small plot to govern; and from the lofty standpoint of heaven there is little to choose between them. When viewed from that exalted height, both patches of earth shrink down to a speck of dust. Likewise our deeds, all those accomplishments that so swell us with pride, what are they? The smallest of them and the greatest are alike cast into insignificance by the measure of the Almighty.

In the end, as the historian insisted, only character counts; not what we have done, but how faithfully we have done it, and why. People can be very busy doing many things, but whether or not they are serving God in all their hurry is another matter. Whose ambition are you fulfilling? Yours or God's? Whose interests are you really serving?

If you fail to discover what God wishes you to do, if you take on a host of projects that lie outside his will, if you set your own agenda without consulting him, then you will soon find life becoming an oppressive burden! By contrast, Jesus declared, *"My yoke is easy and my burden is light."* (Mt 11:30). To serve God wholeheartedly is in the end the only sensible thing to do.

## A CAST-OFF PREACHER

Statistics have scant attraction for God. His focus is not on the pile of beans we have laboured to accumulate, and are so busy counting. We could lose them all without troubling him over much.

---

[18] The French Revolution (first published in 1837) Volume One, Book One: "The Death of Louis XV," Chapter Four.

He is not concerned about the *count*, but the *count-er*. Not *what*, but *who*?

On the day that is coming, you will be assessed not on how well you succeeded in some earthly enterprise, but on how well you succeeded as a *human being*. Even Paul was a little apprehensive about the possibility of failing this test –

> *I beat my body black and blue, and keep it under severe discipline, otherwise I might find that I have preached to others but am cast aside myself (1 Co 9:27).*

Can a great and highly successful preacher find that his glorious work has all been for nothing? Yes, if he forgets that God does not care nearly so much about what he has *done* as about who he *is*.

So your works and mine, including the best and most noble, will have value on the Day of Judgment only insofar as they show the kind of person we are, and especially how well we reflect the character of Christ.

This equality of destiny matched with the unpredictable vicissitudes of life should make any attentive person wary of putting too much hope in material things (see Mt 6:19-20; Lu 12:32-34). The grave consumes monarchs as readily as merchants; death has no favourites, makes no distinctions, and treats all human differences with disdain. As Horace said in one of his famous *Odes* (I.iv.13) –

> *Pale Death kicks his way equally into the cottages of the poor and the castles of kings.*

Similarly, each new day is fraught with uncertainty, for the highest in the land just as it is for the lowest. A ruler today can be a slave tomorrow, and a pauper may rise to be a king (Ec 4:14-16).

These things are so self-evident it is amazing that anyone ever forgets them. Yet since most of us do forget, many prophets and divines, sages and poets, have striven to remind us of them, and to scourge the folly of loving this chancy world too much.

O sudden grief that ever art near neighbour
To worldly bliss! Sprinkled with bitterness
The ends of joy in all our earthly labour!
Grief occupies the goal to which we press.
For your own safety think it is no less,
And in your day of gladness bear in mind
The unknown evil forging on behind! [19]

## OUR HOPE MUST BE IN CHRIST

I once heard Billy Graham say that no one is ready to live until he
or she is first ready to die. Is that a paradox of despair? No, for
while I know that I must die, I also know that Christ has triumphed
over the grave – therefore I shall never die! Death has lost its sting,
the grave has lost its victory! Now, in the freedom of Christ, each
new day weaves its richest texture, and each hour builds its most
joyous frame.

Is that how the fabric of your life is woven? Are these things its
warp and woof? Is your heart fixed on obtaining *"the prize of the
high calling of God in Christ"*? Are you living for eternal values,
ready for this world because you are ready for the next? Are you fit
to live because you know how to die? Has earth become precious
because heaven is more so? Are your possessions here touched
with grace because your true affections are fixed above, where
Christ is, sitting at the right hand of God?

I do not see how anyone living in such a golden setting could ever
lapse into dejection. Surely there is here an admirable cure for the
bleakest depression, a panacea for the most melancholy soul,
medicine to cheer the dullest heart! We're on the way to heaven.
Christ awaits our coming. The angels are ready to herald our

[19] The Canterbury Tales, by Geoffrey Chaucer (1345-1400); tr. by Nevill
Coghill; Penguin Classics, 1977; pg. 151.

arrival with a thunder of acclamation. What is there in this brief moment of earthly existence that could possibly cloud such indestructible joy?

---

## POINTS TO PONDER

➢ What does this statement mean? "We are not so much people of today as people of tomorrow!"

➢ What is meant by the saying, "develop the fine art of seeing the invisible"?

➢ Do you agree with the saying that the only lasting edifice we can build is to fix our souls in the hearts of other people?

➢ Why is it that in the end what will count will not be what we have done but who we are?

➢ Ponder the saying that no one is ready to live until he or she is first ready to die.

## CHAPTER FIVE:

# RESISTING PROVIDENCE

Do you wish to be counted among the wise? Then find contentment in the way God has ordered your life. Few people are really contented with their lot; most of us feel that if God had bothered to ask our opinion, things would have been arranged rather differently! So we don't hesitate to push and pull and twist and turn until we have secured what we consider a more congenial state of affairs. Sometimes it works out well, but so seldom that most counsellors (including John the Baptist, Lu 3:14), have urged people to make the best of where they are and what they have. Struggling to gain more possessions or a higher status rarely opens a door to happiness –

> *Do not press the Lord to promote you to some high office . . . Do not seek to become a judge, for you may find that you cannot root out injustice, or you may be overwhelmed by some great person and so mar your integrity (Sirach 7:4-7).*

The rabbi does not mean, of course, that no one should ever aspire to be a judge, or try to gain high office; rather, he is warning against craving a role that may be beyond your ability. Are you strong enough to resist the intimidating face of high rank? Can you cope with the pressures that promotion will bring? Do you tremble before the faces of the rich and powerful? Could you handle sensibly an accession of wealth?

## ALL POWER CORRUPTS

Remember my account above about the misery that destroys many people who come suddenly into great wealth. Few lottery winners ever gain the happiness they expected from their unearned riches. Only a handful manage to build a new level of happiness and prosperity for themselves. Most soon find themselves ruined, their money gone, their families shattered, their friends soured, their lives embittered.

Similarly, many excellent sergeants upon changing their stripes for a lieutenant's pips have been crushed by the extra weight. And many a fine lower-level manager has found only a death sentence in promotion to executive office.

Consider also authority. Do you have enough character to resist the temptations of authority? As the British politician Lord Acton said in 1857, in a letter to a bishop: *"Power tends to corrupt, and absolute power corrupts absolutely."* Authority has turned many a kindly person into a merciless autocrat, hateful to themselves and to all who deal with them. Indeed, it is doubtful if anyone can altogether resist the corrupting tendency that seems to accompany any possession by one person of authority over another.

## GODLINESS WITH CONTENTMENT

So while he does not actually forbid us to be ambitious for better things, Jesus nonetheless insists that we should be generally contented with our place in life (Mt 6:25-34*)*. If you have food, clothing, housing, what do you have to be worried about? (He 13:5-6). For a more diverse happiness, other things may be highly desirable, but not if they demand from you fretting distress, anxious toil, restless struggle.

Now this wisdom is not hidden in a corner. The same good sense has been spoken by countless sages across the centuries. It stands also in many places on the pages of scripture, where it is reinforced by an inescapable demand to yield to the will of God.

Here are a few selections, both from the Bible and from other literature. You would do well to meditate on them –

> *Religion is a source of enormous benefit, but only for people who are content with their lot. We brought nothing into this world, and we can take*

*nothing out of it. Do you have food and clothing? Then what more do you need? Anyone who craves riches will face many temptations and will have to cope with many snares. Such foolish and ruinous ambitions plunge people into destruction (1 Ti 6:6-10).*

In those words of advice to Timothy, Paul says nothing new. In fact he was only echoing the similar counsel given by Sirach to his young disciples, some 200 years earlier –

*The real necessities of life are simple: water, bread, clothing, and a house for the sake of privacy. The life of a poor man, living under his own roof, is better than endless banqueting in the house of another. So learn how to be content, whether you have little or much. . . . If you crave riches your life will never be pleasing, for the pursuit of money will always take you onto a wrong path.*

*How many people have been ruined by gold! They hoped for happiness, but instead found themselves face to face with destruction! Those who turn gold into a god cannot escape being pulled down into the Pit. What fools they are to be ensnared by it! Are there any rich people who are still blameless? How happy they are if they have not let gold become the beacon of their lives! (Sirach 29:21-23; 31:5-11).*

Do not imagine that the rabbi and Paul were talking only about gold in a literal sense. Rather, they were scolding any insatiable hunger for more – whether more money, more success, more applause, or more of anything that belongs only to this world. Their admonition is just as applicable to a frustrated pastor hungering for a bigger congregation as to a frustrated businessman yearning for larger profits. Skulking in the shadows of all restless human ambition there is a golden idol.

## CONTENTED WITH YOUR LOT

Now let Paul speak again, warning about the bizarre folly of thinking you know better than God what is right for you –

> *Would you dare answer back to God? Can a lump of clay say to a potter, "Why are you making me into this shape?" Surely the potter has every right to turn the clay into any shape he pleases? Why, from the very same lump he can make two different pots, one beautiful and the other common! (Ro 9:20-21).*

Remember how caustically Moses rebuked the Levites who were not content with their station, but wanted a more important position –

> *It should be enough for you that the God of Israel has taken you out from among the people and set you apart for his service. How great is your privilege! You stand before God to minister in the Tabernacle of the Lord, and you stand before the people as the ministers of the congregation. . . . Yet now you would seek the priesthood as well! Indeed, you and all your company have conspired together against the Lord. (Nu 16:8-11)*

Our prayer should rather be that of the poet –

My goal is God himself, not joy, nor peace,
Nor even blessing, but himself, my God:
'Tis his to lead me there, not mine, but his –
"At any cost, dear Lord, by any road!"
So faith bounds forward to its goal in God,

And love can trust her Lord to lead her there;
Upheld by him, my soul is following hard,
Till God hath full fulfilled my deepest prayer. [20]

## IN THE WRONG PLACE?

Refusing to heed poets and prophets, many people remain discontented with their lot in life and fall into a morass of self-pity. They once expected prosperity and happiness, and now cannot understand why so many of their hopes have turned sour. But we must recognise that disappointment is part of the fibre of life –

> *Actors are so fortunate. They can choose whether they will appear in a tragedy or a comedy, whether they will suffer or make merry, laugh or shed tears. But in real life it is different. Most men and women are forced to perform parts for which they have no qualifications. . . . The world is a stage, but the play is badly cast.* [21]

Have you ever felt like that? The wrong person in the wrong place doing the wrong thing at the wrong time? It is a common experience –

> ➢ We shall generally find that the triangular person has gone into the square hole, the oblong into the triangular, and the square person has squeezed himself into the round hole. The officer and the office, the doer and the thing done, seldom fit so exactly that we can say they were almost made for each other. [22]

---

[20] F. Brook.

[21] Oscar Wilde, Lord Arthur Savile's Crime, Chapter One.

[22] From Sketches of Moral Philosophy, by Sydney Smith (1771-1845), English clergyman, essayist, and wit.

Few of us feel truly fitted for the role we are called upon to play. Most people, if they were free to do so, would choose to be someone different, or to work in a different job, or to own different things – in a word, to have a life other than the one they are obliged to live.

In 1457 the French duke of Orleans (who spent 25 years in England as an unwilling hostage) composed the line, *"I am dying of thirst by the side of the fountain,"* and he offered a handsome prize for the best ballad to use that line. The duke died, and his prize remained unclaimed; but in 1961 the poet Richard Purdy Wilbur wrote –

> Duke, keep your coin.
> All men are born distraught,
> And will not for the world be satisfied.
> Whether we live in fact, or but in thought,
> We die of thirst, here at the fountain side.

That is indeed the normal human condition: we are all in some sense like that man dying of thirst while a fountain sparkles beside him. We are a people craving what we cannot obtain, ever hunting for magical pots of gold at the end of illusory rainbows. A people "born distraught" who "will not for the world be satisfied". No wonder so many succumb to depression!

The question is, what will you do about it? You can stay in that bleak condition if you prefer; or you can escape it. How? By letting the gospel teach you two things –

## 1) KNOWLEDGE OF THE UNIVERSAL SAVIOUR

Many things are true of our Saviour, but this is perhaps the most marvellous of all: *Jesus satisfies!* He is the balm of Gilead, the water of life, the bread of heaven, the well of salvation.

Can anyone drink deeply from this well, yet still thirst? (Jn 4:10-14). At his right hand there are pleasures for evermore (Ps 16:11). Whatever is touched by his grace is transformed.

The young Canadian poet Robert Service, unable to sleep one April night in 1914, got up and looked through the window of his 5<sup>th</sup>-floor Parisian garret. The squalid slums stretched out beneath his gaze, yet they were painted by the soft moonlight, and changed into

> . . . a silver city rapt and still;
> Dim, drowsy deeps of opal haze,
> And spire and dome in diamond blaze;
> The little lisping leaves of spring
> Like sequins softly glimmering;
> Each roof a plaque of argent sheen,
> A gauzy gulf the space between;
> Each chimney top a thing of grace,
> While merry moonbeams prank and chase;
> And all that sordid was and mean,
> Just Beauty, deathless and serene. [23]

In the same way, Christ changes the aspect of life for every person who is in true union with him. Everything is made different. What was ugly becomes lovely, what was mundane becomes heavenly, what was natural becomes spiritual –

> Heav'n above is softer blue,
> Earth around is sweeter green;
> Something lives in ev'ry hue
> Christless eyes have never seen;
> Birds with gladder songs o'erflow,
> Flowers with deeper beauties shine,
> Since I know, as now I know,
> I am his and he is mine. [24]

---

[23] Ballads of a Bohemian; Book One, "Spring", 'Insomnia'; T. Fisher Unwin, London, 1921; pg. 31.

[24] G. Wade Robinson.

Has that been your experience of Christ? Or are you still dying of thirst beside the Fountain of Living Water? Perhaps you need to trust him more, or yield more fully to him? Or perhaps you need to add another dimension to your faith?

However, to know Christ as the Universal Saviour is incomplete unless you also discover some –

## 2)  KNOWLEDGE OF OUR UNIVERSAL DESTINY

We are like the passengers and crew on a ship, each with a different berth, but all heading for the same harbour and the same joys. On that far shore the differences that seemed so important on the ship will vanish. There the least may be great, and the great may be least!

Shipboard distinctions are important only during a voyage. What really counts is the status each passenger will have when they all disembark in their new land. There the captain, who was so important while the voyage lasted, may have little status; while some unnoticed passengers may actually be the holders of high national office. Thus a lively vision of heaven, and of the permanent bliss that awaits us there, is a powerful antidote to the passing blues of the present time!

## POINTS TO PONDER

➢ Is it possible for anyone to remain wholly untarnished by the corrupting tendency that arises from taking authority over someone else?

➢ What sort of ambition does the above chapter condemn, and what sort (if any) does it commend?

➢ Can God be said to deal fairly with us when most of us feel, at least sometimes, that we are like a square peg being rammed into a round hole?

➢ How does the knowledge of Christ change the aspect of everything in life?

➢ In what way does knowledge of the destiny God has appointed for us in Christ add a new and dynamic dimension to every event?

CHAPTER SIX:

# DISCOVER WHO YOU ARE

The surging sea of human life forever onward rolls,
And bears to the eternal shore its daily freight of souls;
Though bravely sails our bark today, pale Death sits at the prow,
And few shall know we ever lived, a hundred years from now.

Why should we try so earnestly in life's short, narrow span,
On golden stairs to climb so high above our brother man?
Why blindly at an earthly shrine in slavish homage bow?
Our gold will rust, ourselves be dust, a hundred years from now.

Why prize so much the world's applause? Why dread so much
    its blame?
A fleeting echo is its voice of censure or of fame;
The praise that thrills the heart, the scorn that dyes with shame
    the brow,
Will be as long-forgotten dreams a hundred years from now.

Whenever we celebrate too gleefully some personal achievement, it is useful to remember the sobering truth expressed by Mary Ford [25] – *the very greatest of us will be soon forgotten!*

For example, here are four men who changed the world: have you ever heard of them?

## AMENHOTEP IV

Perhaps the first monotheistic monarch in history, Amenhotep, pharaoh of Egypt, flourished in the $14^{th}$ century BC ($18^{th}$ dynasty).

---

[25] In her poem <u>A Hundred Years From Now</u>. Ironically, she wrote the poem just on 100 years ago, and is herself now virtually forgotten by all!

He renounced the old gods and declared that there could be only one supreme deity in the universe, whom he portrayed under a symbol of the sun, sovereign of the sky. In Egypt the sun was named *aton*, so the pharaoh changed his name to *Akhenaton – "All goes well, with Aton"*. His queen was the beautiful Nefertiti, whose exquisite statue still survives. On his death, he was succeeded by the young Tutankhamen, whose tomb was discovered in 1922 by Lord Carnarvon and Howard Carter, causing a worldwide sensation. Akhenaton defaced or erased every image he could find of the ancient deities, and tried to establish his new religion in the land by moving his capital from Thebes to a site 300 kilometres north, which he called Akhetaton (*"Horizon of Aton"* – now called Tell el Amarna). Some of his writings have survived, including a beautiful psalm, which bears a striking resemblance to the biblical *Psalm 104* (although it is unlikely that either psalm directly influenced the other). Akhenaton's psalm begins –

> How glorious in beauty you are
> When you appear on the edge of heaven,
> O thou living Aton, the creator of all life!
> When you rise at dawn over the eastern horizon,
> You fill the whole earth with your splendour.
> How benevolent you are, majestic, brilliant,
> Standing high over every land.
> Your rays embrace the nations, to the furthest limit
> Of all that you have made . . .

He changed the course of history, but few know anything about him today.

## EMPEDOCLES

A Greek philosopher, physician, and political theorist, who flourished during the 5th century BC, Empedocles was so renowned for his brilliance, and for the astonishing breadth and depth of his numerous writings, that he was offered a crown. He declined it, and urged the people instead to consider the benefits of a democracy. It has been said that almost alone he re-shaped the world of his own time, and that his influence still reaches across the centuries into our modern culture. So great was his genius (according to an ancient legend), that he began to feel he must be something more than a mere man, and became anxious about losing prestige if he died in the ordinary way. So to disguise his death, and to create an impression that he had been carried up into heaven and ensconced among the deities on Mount Olympus, he secretly cast himself into the crater of Mt Etna. He supposed that no trace of him would remain and that his friends would all suppose he had undergone a divine apotheosis. Unhappily for his plan, an updraft caught one his sandals, and coughed it onto the side of the volcano, where it was later found. So his friends guessed what he had done, and lamented the folly of one who in other ways had been so wise.

But his influence remained, re-shaping human society. Yet how many today know even his name?

## PHILLIP II

Nearly everybody has heard of Alexander the Great, but how much do you know about his father Phillip? You may, of course, if you are a reader or scholar, know a great deal about him; but to most people he is a complete stranger. Yet beginning as king of Macedon, which was then a barbaric and insignificant nation, he dreamed of uniting the entire Greek world and of spreading its culture, arts, literature, and civilisation to the ends of the earth. By brilliant conquest and impressive diplomacy he swiftly raised Macedon to the status of a major power and gained sovereignty over the Grecian peninsula. Thus he created the first true nation-state in the history of Europe.

Phillip then took the first steps toward overthrowing the Persian Empire, a daring enterprise that was splendidly achieved by his son Alexander. Who knows what Phillip might have achieved if he had not been assassinated (in 336 BC when he was but 54 years old?

Like Empedocles, Phillip enjoyed such extraordinary success that he was in danger of supposing himself more than mortal. Fearful that such pride might ruin him, Phillip arranged for two men to approach him every morning and say, "Phillip, remember that you are but a man!" And then to come to him again in the evening and say, "Phillip, did you remember that you are but a man?"

Alexander his son thoroughly deserved the honour of becoming the first man in history to be awarded the title "Great". But what could Alexander have done if Phillip had not so thoroughly prepared the way? Yet who today bothers to commend Phillip?

## PYRRHUS

King of Epirus in northern Greece (319-272 BC), Pyrrhus was a daring and brilliant military commander. He was one of the few men ever to defeat the Roman legions, which he did twice. At one point in his campaign he approached the very walls of Rome itself, creating terror among its previously invulnerable citizens. Only the onset of winter obliged him to retreat. The Romans, after mustering all their forces, finally defeated him, and he left Italy, never to return. But he kept on enjoying military triumphs in other lands until, laying siege to the city of Argos, he was killed by a tile thrown at him from a roof by a woman. It is said that after one of his Roman victories, which cost him many men, several of his dearest friends and commanders, and all his baggage, that he remarked: "Another victory like that, and we will be ruined!" From which comes the saying, "a pyrrhic victory" – meaning one that cost the victor too high a price.

Pyrrhus changed the shape of history by the upheavals he caused in the fledgling Roman republic, forcing the senators to alter their policy, and to change their military tactics. But to most people today he is completely unknown, and even the once-popular saying built around his name has fallen into disuse.

From all this we are reminded once again that we dare not find our value in what we *do*, but rather in who we *are*. I have already mentioned this idea, but here we look at another aspect of it – not the character we should strive to build within ourselves, but rather, the character built into us by God. See then 1 Peter 2:4-5, 9-10. Each Christian is –

# A DIVINE CREATION

*You are God's own people, and you should be demonstrating the wonderful things he has done!*

Rabbi Eleazar (says an old fable) had reached the end of his life. A group of young men, his disciples, were gathered around the bed, hoping for a last word from their dying master. All was silent, until one of the young men, a little bolder than the others, prompted the rabbi to leave them with a final pearl of wisdom. Again there was silence. Suddenly, the old man stirred, seeming to catch a new surge of life, and sat up. With some of the former fire sparkling in his eyes, he looked at the disciples and spoke: "My sons, I have learned this above all else. When in a few minutes I stand before my Maker, he will not ask me, "Eleazar, why were you not more like my servant *Abraham*?" Nor will he say, "Why were you not more like my servant *Moses*?" Nor will he say, "Why were you not more like my servant *Joshua*?" Nor will he say, "Why were you not more like my servant *Elijah*? Nor will he ask me why I was not more like *David*, or *Amos*, or *Jeremiah*, or *Ezra*." No! He will ask me only one question: "Eleazar, why were you not more like *Eleazar*?"

There is probably no wiser lesson to learn than this: *God wants you to be yourself, not someone else!* If he had wanted you to be like this spiritual hero or that, or like such a giant of the faith, or like some other glorious warrior, or prophet, or evangelist, or whatever, or whoever, *that is how he would have made you.* He did not. He made *you*! Presumably, he likes what his own hand made!

Our problem is not that we fail to emulate some wonderful saint of the past or present, but that *we fail to emulate ourselves* – that is, we do not live out our own wonderful potential. When God first formed you and me in each mother's womb, he had a beautiful dream of what your life and mine could be – the character we could develop; the loveliness we could display; the strength we could exert; the splendid deeds we could do; the great things we could achieve; the worship we could offer; the maturity we could reach; the prize we could gain.

We can never do better than fulfil that dream the Father has had for each one of us from the very beginning. Live your own life, not someone else's!

# A ROYAL PRIESTHOOD

*You are a chosen race, a holy nation,*
*a royal priesthood.*

We possess the highest status in the universe, below only God himself: we are his *royal priests*. Along with this rank come two marvellous boons –

## 1) THE RIGHT OF FREE ACCESS TO THE THRONE OF GOD

How is this access gained? By some personal merit? Never! Solely by divine grace, and through the blood of the everlasting covenant. No one can earn it. It cannot be bought. No sacrifice, worship, song, prayer, price, or pain, will ever suffice to earn any Christian even one moment's access to the throne. We step up to the throne by grace alone, with faith alone, trusting in the merits of Christ alone, or we will be barred all access.

Yet in worship services, prayer meetings, conferences, seminars, and in Christian books and journals, I constantly meet the idea that there is something *I* must *do*, some effort I must exert, some cost I must meet, before I may hope to advance into the very presence of God. What heresy! Whenever you encounter such sentiments, dismiss them! Give them no patience, offer them no hearing, allow them no residence in your mind or spirit.

The gospel speaks imperatively: *"The way into the holiest is now made open through the blood of Christ!"* Therefore, as the apostle cries,

> *Let us approach the throne of grace boldly, so that we may find grace and mercy to help us in our time of need ... With unwavering confidence we may enter the holiest through the blood of Jesus, by the new and living way that he has himself opened for us ... through his own flesh. . . .(And) let us draw near with a true heart, in full assurance of faith ... holding fast to the confession of our faith without wavering, for he who promised is faithful! (He 4:16; 10:19-23)*

Anything more than this, anything less than this, is not the gospel, but some kind of pious distortion. Let us cast aside all such spurious notions, clinging to the truth as it is in Christ, refusing to be entangled again in some yoke of bondage, insisting on every privilege that belongs to all who are the free-born children of the Lord, the members of his *royal priesthood!*

## 2) THE RIGHT TO SPEAK WITH ROYAL AUTHORITY

Viscount Augustus Keppel (1725-86), when he was but 25 years old, was sent by the British government to Algiers to demand that its prince put an end to Algerian piracy in the Mediterranean. When the dey saw the young viscount he mocked him, demanding how the king of England could dare to send a beardless youth on such a mission. Keppel replied, "Had my master supposed that wisdom was measured by the length of the beard, he would have sent to your highness a goat!"

The dey was enraged, and called upon a soldier to kill the British envoy at once. But Keppel simply pointed through an adjacent window. Through it, the British fleet could be seen, moored just off-shore. Then the young viscount calmly said, "My friends in those ships will ensure that if I die here, your burning palace will make a glorious funeral pyre for us all!" The dey capitulated, and said that he would do as the British demanded.

That anecdote is a fine example of the principle of authority at work. Keppel had no personal *power*, but he did have *authority* – and that authority was backed up by the power of the British sovereign. So too, we have been given royal authority in Christ, to speak against all the dark works of the Enemy, whether of sin or sickness, poverty or failure, or whatever of Satan *"steals, kills, and destroys"* (Jn 10:10).

But authority is worthless unless its holder

### a) KNOWS THAT HE OR SHE POSSESSES IT

Many Christians have never grasped the fact that they *have already* been given royal authority in Christ, to *"tread on serpents and scorpions, and over all the power of the enemy"* (Lu 10:17-20), and that God's intention is to *"crush Satan"*, not under *his* feet, but under *"your feet"*! (Ro 16:20) Authority unknown is authority undone. So, if you have not yet grasped it, awaken now to what Christ has given you, clothe yourself with the mantle of his righteousness, and prepare to *"move mountains"* in his name! (Mk 11:22-24)

Then, *second*, authority is still worthless unless its holder

### b) IS WILLING TO EXERCISE IT

How far would Lord Keppel have got if he had been timid and uncertain, afraid of the Algerian pirate prince, apologetic and unsure of his mandate? Beyond doubt, he would have been at once slaughtered at the dey's command, or, perhaps worse, treated with scorn and jeered out of the palace. He prevailed because he knew who he was, knew what authority he possessed, knew the power that stood behind him, and spoke with bold assurance.

Do you find yourself confronting the dark Pirate Prince of hell? Then do as the viscount did. *Who are you?* A born-again believer in Jesus Christ, and a member of the King's royal family, carrying a nobility much higher than that of any earthly lord. *What authority do you possess?* The authority of Christ himself, who said that *"all power is given to me, in heaven and on the earth"* (Mt 28:18) *What power stands behind you?* Nothing less than the sovereign might of the King of kings and the Lord of lords, along with all the battalions and resources of heaven! *How should you speak against the devil and all his works?* With brave confidence, bold assurance, unwavering faith, strong command, and an unshakeable certainty that what you say will be done.

The one proviso is that we possess authority only to speak in accord with the word of God and in harmony with his will, in his name and not our own. But so long as we are acting in harmony with the divine purpose and promise then we may speak with all the authority that belongs to all who are the true ambassadors of Christ (2 Co 5:20).

## A DESTINED HEIR

*Once you were no-one, but now you belong to God; once you had nothing, but now you have received God's mercy.*

The 19th cent. English satirist W. M. Thackery wrote a spoof (*Rebecca and Rowena*) on Sir Walter Scott's novel *Ivanhoe,* and he said –

*Thus Sir Wilfred of Ivanhoe, having attained the height of his wishes, was, like many a man when he has reached that dangerous elevation, disappointed. Ah, dear friends, it is but too often so in life! Many a garden, seen from a distance, looks fresh and green, which, when beheld closely, is dismal and weedy; the shady walks melancholy and grass-grown; the bowers you would fain repose in, cushioned with stinging nettles. I have ridden in a caique upon the waters of the Bosphorus, and looked upon the capital of the Soldan of Turkey. As seen from those blue waters, with palace and pinnacles, with gilded dome and towering cyprus, it seemeth a very paradise of Mahound: but, enter the city, and it is but a beggarly labyrinth of rickety huts and dirty alleys, where the ways are steep and the smells are foul, tenanted by many dogs and ragged beggars – a dismal illusion! Life is such; oh, well-a-day! It is only hope which is real, and reality is a bitterness and a deceit. (Chapter One)*

We Christians, too, can experience the same bitter disappointments. The privileges, rights, and authority we have in Christ certainly enable us to complete whatever lies in the Father's purpose for us, but they do not shield us from all pain or deprivation. So we may and do experience loss and hurt. Our sweetest dreams may fail. A joy upon which we pinned dear hope may turn sour. A friend may betray us. Some natural disaster may wreck our dreams. Fire, flood, and famine, misfortune and misery, may strike down Christian families as well as their ungodly neighbours. An air disaster, a freeway accident, a ship collision, a train derailment, may destroy Christian lives along with those of the ungodly. We may also be called upon to suffer persecution for the sake of the gospel. Then, at a lesser level, we may find that the happiness we had hoped to gain from this or that seldom equals our anticipation. Life can become as frustrating or as disillusioning for us Christians as for anyone.

But there is this wonderful difference. We who believe in Jesus are protected from despair! Even in this life the darkest hour is lightened by his promise, *"I will never leave you nor forsake you!"* (He 13:5); which enables us to laugh, *"Since the Lord is my helper, I will not be afraid! What harm can anyone do to me?"* (vs. 6). The promise is also true, both today and forever, that *"there is inexhaustible pleasure at God's right hand!"* (Ps 16:11) We cannot help but laugh with Paul, knowing that the troubles of this present time are not worth noticing when they are placed alongside the magnificence that will one day be ours in Christ! (2 Co 4:16-18; Ro 8:18)

# CONCLUSION

None of these things will happen of their own accord. So in partnership with Christ let us set about finding and living-out our own true selves. We should do this in the spiritual authority of Christ; never looking back, but always pressing on toward the splendid prize that belongs to the high calling God has given us in Christ (Ph 3:12-15).

**POINTS TO PONDER**

➤ Try to obtain (perhaps from your local library) a copy of Akhenaton's *Psalm,* and then compare it with the biblical *Psalm 104.*

➤ Can you think of other people who changed the course of history but are now mostly unknown?

➤ How does the statement *"be yourself"* blend with that other equally (and perhaps more) important statement *"be like Jesus"*?

➤ In what way does the atoning death of Christ provide the only key that can unlock the otherwise closed door into the presence of God?

➤ If we Christians are just as much subject to misfortune as our ungodly neighbours, what advantages *do* we have that they lack?

*CHAPTER SEVEN:*

# MADE IN GOD'S IMAGE

*Text: "Let us make human beings in our image"* *(Ge 1:26-27).*

You probably know that potatoes and yams resemble each other. A preacher once used some potatoes as object lessons in a sermon, in which he likened them to people in the church – *dic-tater; agi-tater; imi-tater*; etc. He summed up by urging them all to be *sweet-taters*. On the way out, one of his parishioners responded, "I yam what I yam!" (Reader's Digest)

But what really am I? Scripture says that we are God's people, *"made in his **image** and after his **likeness**."* But what does *that* mean?

Commentators vary in their lists, but commonly the divine image in us is thought to consist of a –

> *moral nature*
> *spiritual essence*
> *reasoning mind*
> *power of speech*
> *creative skill.*

But here is a rather different list –

## WE LAUGH AT A JOKE

*"He who sits enthroned in the heavens laughs!"* (Ps 2:4)

According to Dr R. B. Zajonc, professor of psychology at the University of Michigan, when you smile, your facial muscles push against the veins and arteries in your head. This changes the amount of blood that flows into your brain, which then affects the production of some powerful brain chemicals called neuro-transmitters. These remarkable chemicals are able to kill pain and to brighten your mood. It reminds one of the scripture, *"Better even than medicine, a merry heart will do you good!"* (Pr 17:22).

This leads me to say that one of the weirdest ideas ever to grip Christians has been the notion that laughter is impious. Yet, despite scores of biblical references to joy, gladness, and merriment, some gloomily pious people want to banish the sound of laughter from Christian life and from the church.

But laughter is unique to human beings. It is part of the divine image in us. God laughs, therefore we laugh. No angel can appreciate a good joke. They must wonder at our amusement, unable to discern why we think something is so funny. Nor can any other creature appreciate humour. Try telling a joke to your dog! Show a cartoon to your cat! Ask a parrot to appreciate a punch-line! How foolish! In the entire creation, both on earth and in heaven, only humans laugh; and among humans, *only we Christians have any reason to laugh*!

For example, here is an ungodly man and an impious woman. Nothing lies ahead for these people except death, the grave, and the judgment of heaven. You wonder what could ever bring laughter to their lips. Endless tears would seem more appropriate (Ja 5:1; Mt 8:12; 22:13; 24:51; 25:30; Lu 13:28; Ja 4:9; etc.) That people who have no hope of heaven, but only the certainty of everlasting ruin, can and do still laugh is a witness of how powerfully this divine likeness is built into us. Indeed, humour is so deeply rooted in the human spirit that almost nothing can entirely obliterate it.

Whatever may be true of others, we Christians have abundant reasons to make merry. As the apostle says, because we believe, we can and should *"rejoice with joy unspeakable and full of glory!"* (1 Pe 1:8, KJV).

## WE CREATE BY SPEAKING

Nothing so marks the divine likeness in us as the power of speech. Its origin is inexplicable; its qualities are unique. No sociological, biological, or educational theory is able to account for the existence of human speech. Truly, one of the most baffling mysteries of human life is our ability to communicate with words. Is this merely a learned skill, or is it innate? Is it just a mechanistic process, or does it reflect something deeply fundamental to what it means to be human? [26]

For many years linguists believed that infants learned how to talk solely by trial and error. That comfortable notion has now been dispelled. Few linguists today doubt that our capacity for language is an implanted thing. They observe that all human languages are governed by a *genetically determined* universal grammar, which is present in every normal child at birth.

What is the origin of this native sense of grammar?

Outside the biblical explanation (that our power of speech is a gift from God) the question cannot find an adequate answer.

So the evidence strongly suggests that language is not just a collection of imitated sounds, but rather depends upon "an innate knowledge of linguistic structure that is part of the genetic birthright of any normal child." [27] Language, therefore, is not just a product of environment, [28] but is inherent in the very fibre of our being.

## HOW DO WE LEARN TO TALK?

These ideas can be illustrated by asking how children learn to talk. The obvious reply, that they copy their parents and siblings, falls

---

[26] The paragraphs that follow, dealing with the marvel of speech, are adapted from my book <u>Strong Reasons.</u>

[27] John L. Casti, <u>Paradigms Lost</u>; Cardinal Books, London 1989; pg. 212.

[28] Except, of course, that cultural factors obviously determine *which* language a person speaks.

under the objection of "a poverty of stimulus" (as Casti calls it). That is, "the child is not exposed to enough language to account for the linguistic ability displayed by any normal six-year old. In short, children's ability to use their native language is vastly under-determined by the data." [29]

What are those data?

Snatches of conversation, "baby talk", ill-formed words and sentences, half-stated ideas, all mixed up with careful speech, incomplete statements, questions, nonsense words, teasing, and the like. Yet out of it all, a child swiftly emerges with an ability to construct sentences that he or she has never heard before.

## AN INSTINCT FOR GRAMMAR

Further, the child instinctively masters grammar, and is able, without being aware of it, to apply rules of grammar to new sentences, along with a sensitivity to humour, sarcasm, ambiguity, and other subtle speech factors. And all this occurs in contexts in which the child has never before heard such expressions!

Little of that remarkable ability can be attributed to imitation. Instead it seems undeniably to arise from catalysts that are built into each child's very genes. It is not just an invention of the human mind, but is inseparable from those factors that irrevocably set men and women apart from all other creatures. No animal can ever be taught to speak; yet an infant does so without effort. A child's inborn capacity to recognise, and even more to produce grammatically correct and meaningful sentences, is part of the image of God in each person. It is a phenomenon for which no merely physical, mechanical, sociological, or evolutionary explanation is adequate. But once we accept the testimony of

---

[29]  Ibid. pg. 216

*Genesis* then the problem is removed. God speaks. We are made in his likeness. Therefore we speak!

## GOD CREATES BY SPEAKING

The *first* thing the Bible tells us about God, is that he speaks: *"God said, 'Let there be . . . !'"* [30] The *second* thing it tells us, is that the first man and woman were made in the likeness of God – that is, in the likeness of a God **who creates by the spoken word**. Echoes of that original act of creation still sound whenever a person speaks today, especially when imagination and creativity lie behind the spoken word.

God has planted in humanity an ability to change things, to create, to destroy, to build, **simply by speaking.** These skills are echoes of our divine semblance, and they appear to be uniquely human. Apparently not even the holy angels possess such attributes of imagination and creativity. As far as we know, no angel can *"move mountains"* simply by commanding them to shift! No angel can emulate God's practice of *"calling those things that are not as though they are"* (Ro 4:17) – but to the man or woman of faith, nothing is more natural than to speak things into and out of existence! (vs. 19-21; He 11:1-3, 6; Ja 5:17; etc).

In the whole creation, then, it would seem that **God has shared his creative word only with men and women**. Out of this creative word all human achievement ultimately arises; without it, we would truly be little more than naked apes.

Furthermore, it was originally God's intention that the human voice should possess not only *creative* power but also *controlling* power. God told his people to go out and to *"subdue"* the earth, and to have *"dominion"* over all it contained (Ge 1:28-30). How

---

[30] This paragraph, and those that immediately follow, on the spoken word of faith, are adapted from my book Faith Dynamics.

was this control to be exercised? Not by *"sweat"* and *"toil"*, for that kind of laborious dominion arose out of God's judgment on our fallen state (Ge 3:17-19). But if not by mechanical contrivance and by our own efforts, then the only method of control remaining to us is that used by God – ***the authority of the spoken word***. Note how Adam and Eve, simply by speaking in the name of God, were able to govern their world and so fulfil the purpose of God. Admittedly, that original dominion was almost entirely destroyed by sin; but it has been restored in a measure to all who are part of the *"new creation"* that God has created in Christ. To us who believe, the voice of faith has been given again, and by that voice we can accomplish every good work the Father commands us to do.[31]

## AUSONIUS AND CAESAR

When Ausonius, a Roman civil servant, was accused of boasting about his ability to perform a difficult task, he cried, "Why should I say that I cannot do what Caesar says I can do?" He thought that true modesty forbade him to plead inability when his king had reckoned him able. [32]

So too should we be bold to assert the truth of *all* that scripture says about us in Christ, and especially about our ability to imitate the creative fiats of God. Did not Jesus himself declare that we could do the impossible simply by speaking boldly in faith? (See Mk 11:22-24; Mt 17:20-21; 21:21-22; Lu 17:5-6.)

---

[31] I am not saying that Adam and Eve had no work to do with their hands. They were after all put into the Garden of Eden *"to till it and keep it"* (Ge. 2:15); but their work was to be a pleasurable and creative expression of faith, not a substitute for it. The spoken word of authority was meant to put a divine dynamic into the work of their hands. We too must employ every skill and strength God has given us; but we too are called to add divine resources to all that we do by the right use of the spoken word of faith.

[32] Boswell, Life of Johnson, Autumn 1747.

# WE YEARN TO WORSHIP

The Peak is high and flush'd
　　At his highest with sunrise fire;
The Peak is high, and the stars are high,
　　And the thought of a man is higher.
A deep below the deep,
　　And a height beyond the height!
Our hearing is not hearing,
　　And our seeing is not sight.

– Alfred, Lord Tennyson, The Voice and the Peak; st. 8 & 9

There is more splendour and divinity in the human spirit than in all the mountain's grandeur, or in the wonders of the starry sky, or in the mysteries of the ocean's depth. There is a matrix in our hearts designed for occupancy only by God, without whom life remains dully empty. Our best hearing and seeing is not done with our natural faculties but with the eyes and ears of the soul. They alone can catch the supernal vision and fill us with the splendour of heaven.

We are made to worship, nor can we help doing so. The question is not whether people do or don't worship – for everyone bows before some god – but rather, where their delight is found. In the end, however, no worship deserves the name, nor can it satisfy, unless it is directed toward the one Living God. All else is idolatry.

Yet worship is like a tender orchid – it may be easily crushed by the clamour of the world. It must be carefully nurtured as our highest gift and sweetest joy, the ultimate origin of all true happiness. Those who forget to worship will be obliged to weep. But out of true worship springs of living water will arise to banish all thirst, energy to surmount every difficulty, and joy to dispel every dark shadow (cp. Jn 4:13-14, 23-24, and notice how the flowing well of eternal life is linked with true worship).

# WE CAN SEE TOMORROW

*"What is man, if his chief good and market of his time be but to sleep and feed? A beast, no more."* [33]

Perhaps the sorriest aspect of modern life is that people have lost the capacity to see beyond today. Yet this faculty is a major divide between us and the animals.

Christians should have a double vision –

*(1)  in this life: a set of goals*

*(2)  in the next life: a crown of gold*

Think about those things, and don't allow yourself to be tricked by the subtle deceits of the enemy!

The use of pigeons to carry messages was unknown in Europe until the time of the Crusades, when the Crusaders observed the Turks using them. On one occasion, in 1124, the Christian army was besieging the city of Tyre, whose inhabitants were hoping for the arrival of a relieving army. A pigeon carrying news that reinforcements were on the way fell into the Christian camp. They at once replaced the message with another, saying that no rescue was forthcoming, and that the city should surrender forthwith. Then they sent the bird on its way again. The disheartened Tyrians waved a flag of surrender and opened their gates to the besieging army.

So we too may be deceived by a false message from the enemy.

---

[33]  <u>Hamlet</u>, 4.4.33.

Later, the Turks tried the same trick on a Christian city, but the forgery was recognised. [34]

So we too should recognise Satan's blandishments and falsehoods and stand firm in faith upon the promises of God.

## WE LOVE OUR NEIGHBOUR

In Tennyson's poem *Maud* the main character is a young man who is slowly succumbing to insanity. He eventually fights his way back to mental health, but early in the poem he expresses a yearning, which we all share, to love and be loved –

O, let the solid ground
Not fail beneath my feet
Before my life has found
What some have found so sweet!
*Then let come what may,*
*What matter if I go mad,*
*I shall have had my day.*
Let the sweet heavens endure,
Not close and darken above me
Before I am quite sure
That there is one to love me!
*Then let come what may*
*To a life that has been so sad,*
*I shall have had my day.* (XI.1,2)

The church is a temple of love. If it is not that, it is nothing. To us, above all others, has come the divine gift that makes us kin to God, which is that of loving and of being loved. Unless we truly exemplify the love of Christ, our profession of faith becomes an

---

[34] From Chronicles of the Crusades ; ed. Elizabeth Hallam; Weidenfeld and Nicolson, London, 1989; pg. 268.

empty pretence (Jn 13:34-35). All great accomplishments, all signs and wonders, all fame and honour, all our works and endeavours, all sacrifice and service, if done apart from practising the love of Christ, are hollow mockeries. Nothing else in our lives will be measured on the Day of Judgment before this is weighed, and if love is lacking, everything else will be discarded (1 Co 13:1-3).

But we are made for love! How then can it be too hard? Nothing should be more natural to a Spirit-filled believer than to display the loving fruit of the Spirit (Ga 5:22). Let us but walk in the Spirit, yielding to his gentle persuasion, to his gracious influence, and love cannot help but blossom in all its radiant beauty.

## CONCLUSION

Don't accept either Satan's or the world's evaluation of your life. We Christians are both God's *creation* and also his *new creation* – doubly made in his image and likeness!

Therefore –

> ➤ you should highly honour *yourself*; and
> ➤ we should highly honour *each other*.

In these things lies a prescription for a more joyful life, free from the dreads that often crush human happiness.

## POINTS TO PONDER

➢ Would you have chosen laughter as a primary mark of the divine image in human beings? If not, why not?

➢ If human speech has creative power, does this mean that *every* word we speak, whether idle or deliberate, has some natural or spiritual impact? Can there exist such a thing as *neutral* speech, that is, words that have no effect, whether good or bad?

➢ If worship is an ineradicable instinct of the human spirit, it behooves each of us to ask ourselves frequently: *"Who or what am I presently worshipping?"*

➢ If the church is failing in its missionary mandate, what is the main cause? A lack of evangelistic effort? Or perhaps rather a lack of true Christian love?

*CHAPTER EIGHT:*

# FALSE VALUES

*There are three precious things which I prize and hold fast. The first is gentle compassion; the second is economy; the third is humility, not presuming to take precedence in the world. With gentle compassion I can be brave. With economy I can be liberal. Not presuming to take precedence in the world, I can make myself a vessel fit for the most distinguished services. Nowadays they give up gentle compassion, and cultivate mere physical courage; they give up economy, and try to be lavish without it; they give up being last, and seek to be first – of all which, the end is death.* [35]

Here is a common cause of depression: *a false sense of values.* People expect *things* that can never do so to bring them personal fulfilment. Or they value themselves by the number of their possessions. Or they build their identity on the work they do, and how much they have achieved. Those are all false measures. God prizes *spiritual* not *material* objects; he seeks *character* more than *achievement*. We need to find value where God finds it.

## CHILDREN OR EMPLOYEES?

Here is another way to look at it: God wants to call us children, not workers; he wants to relate to us as our Father, not as our boss. Think about this: one of your children may start working for you; but will you therefore value him more than other children who are

---

[35] Lao Tse, op. cit., pg. 47-48.

employed by someone else? Surely you will love them for who they *are*, not for what they *do,* and even less for what they do for wages! Has the Father accepted you in Christ? Then you should accept yourself. Does he value you for how well you have *done*, or for how good you *are*? Is it your *performance* or your *person* that he admires?

Surely just asking such questions is enough to make the answer self-evident.

Why should you look at yourself through any other eyes than the Father's? It is enough that we should see ourselves as God sees us, and to find pleasure simply knowing that he is pleased.

## PRECIOUS LITTLE THINGS

How often too, we fail to see the limitless wealth around us –

> Perhaps you're counted with the Great;
> You strain and strive with mighty men;
> Your hand is on the helm of State;
> Colossus-like you stride . . . and then
> There comes a pause, a shining hour,
> A dog that leaps, a hand that clings:
> O Titan, turn from pomp and power;
> Give all your heart to Little Things.

> I sometimes wonder, after all,
> Amid this tangled web of fate,
> If what is great may not be small,
> And what is small may not be great.
> So wondering I go my way,
> Yet in my heart contentment sings . . .

> O may I ever see, I pray,

God's grace and love in Little Things . . .

Take wealth, take fame, but leave to me,
O Lord of Life, just Little Things. [36]

It is hard to be depressed while a lovely sunset can still grip you with ecstasy, or a child's tiny hand can fill you with awe. How can gloom crush anyone whose spirit still rises on wings of adoration when it sees a gaily fluttering butterfly, or hears a magpie's rapturous song? What darkness of soul can endure the radiant impact of an exquisite rose, or the mysterious wonder of an evening silhouette? If you are too busy to take time to rejoice in such "little things" then you are simply too busy.

Can you witness a majestic thunder storm, and not be moved to worship? Can you hear a baby's laugh and not chuckle with delight? Can you watch the crashing waves or view the mountain's grandeur, and your heart remain unstirred? Then you are engrossed with what is least and have lost God's highest gifts.

In 1927 two friends, Lew Brown and George Gard, composed a song that became world-famous. One line from it is now an English proverb –

And love can come to everyone,
The best things in life are free!

That is, money alone cannot buy them. Indeed, nothing that money can buy has any value alongside the things it cannot buy: the joy of a sweetheart's embrace; the delight of a child's fierce hug; the rhapsody of life itself; and above all, the love of God so freely offered in Christ. That is why Paul was able to say (in a passage I have already quoted), that if we have food and clothing we should

---

[36] Robert Service, op. cit., "The Joy of Little Things", st. 2 & 4, and the last two lines (May 1914); pg. 52.

be happy, especially if love is added to the package. What else do we really need?

---

**POINTS TO PONDER**

➤ What implications could we draw from the similarity between the moral teaching of Lao Tse (*c.* 600 B.C.) and those of the New Testament.

➤ All of us are prone to value ourselves more by what we do, or by what we achieve, than by whom we are. We need to apply this rule to ourselves from time to time, and thus guard against falling under the sway of a false measure of our worth.

➤ How many "little things" have you allowed to bring you rapturous joy today? Do you find in such things many of the chief treasures of life?

CHAPTER NINE:

# TRUE PROSPERITY

Scripture speaks vigorously about the uncertainty that besets each new day (Ja 4:14-16; Ec 9:1,11-12; 11:6).

What shall we do with those statements? Deny them? Ignore them? Emulate the ostrich with its head in the sand?

Surely it is wiser to take account of the unavoidable vicissitudes of life, and to prepare yourself to be strong in the face of both fortune and misfortune –

> *Consider the work of God. Can you straighten what he has made crooked? So in a time of prosperity you should be happy; but if adversity strikes you, then consider this: God has made the one as well as the other, so that you cannot tell what each day will produce.*
>
> *Indeed, during my own futile life I have seen every variety, from righteous people dying in the midst of their righteousness, to the wicked growing old in their wickedness" (Ec 7:13-15).*

How often the wisdom of those lines has been confirmed! Surely you have seen this yourself: unexpected and unwanted things happening in the lives of people around you? Six hundred years ago, so did Geoffrey Chaucer. He drew on the fables of the ancient Greeks, which tell how the hero Hercules climbed to great heights, only to fall precipitately to the depths of misery. In his re-telling of the story, Chaucer took an opportunity to warn his readers to keep a light touch on this world. It may be here today but gone tomorrow! –

> Thus fell the famous, mighty Hercules!
> Who then may trust the dice, at Fortune's throw?

Who joins in worldly struggles such as these
Will be, when least prepared for it, laid low!
Wise is the man who well has learnt to know
Himself. Beware! When Fortune would elect
To trick a man, she plots his overthrow
By such a means as he would least expect. [37]

So it may happen to anyone. Those who are high may fall, while those who are low may find themselves exalted. Shall we then plunge into a pit of despondency? Of course not! How could any child of God become negative, sour, parsimonious, dark with pessimism? Rather we who believe must be, can only be, full of high expectations from both ourselves and from God.

## THE LORD'S PRAYER

Think about the *Lord's Prayer*, how each declaration is unwaveringly positive, confidently affirmative. Nothing bleak, defeatist, nor poor-spirited. And that is how we should pray each day, said Jesus. Here it is, in the familiar words of the *King James Version* –

*Our Father, which art in heaven,*
*Hallowed be thy name.*
*Thy kingdom come.*
*Thy will be done in earth, as it is in heaven.*
*Give us this day our daily bread.*
*And forgive us our debts, as we forgive our debtors.*
*And lead us not into temptation, but deliver us from*

---

[37] The Canterbury Tales – "The Monk's Tale – 'Hercules'"; tr. by Nevill Coghill; Penguin Classics, 1977; pg. 211. In the tale, Hercules, the Greek hero renowned for his "Twelve Labours", was given a poisoned shirt by a woman. Rather than perish by a woman's hand, he took his own life. The Monk told a series of stories, all with the same moral: *fortune and fame remain uncertain even for the best and greatest of mortals.*

*evil:*
*For thine is the kingdom, and the power, and the*
*glory,*
*For ever. Amen! (Mt 6:9-13).*

There the Master teaches us to pray for, and each day to expect cheerfully –

> ➤ the providential care of the Father

> ➤ his divine supply

> ➤ sustenance, bounty and blessing

> ➤ his pardoning grace and victory; and

> ➤ an outworking of all the dynamics of the kingdom of God in our lives.

What else is that if not a recipe for excitement, fulfilment, joy, and true prosperity?

Once again, those are the things we should wake up each morning expecting from the Father's hand. If so, how could anyone start the day depressed?

## THE SHEPHERD PSALM

Watch the psalmist, as he finds himself stumbling through the dark valley of the shadow of death. What will he do? Fall into despair? No, he reaches out for the comfort of God, and allows no dread to enter his mind. Instead, he expresses unshakeable confidence that he will soon emerge from darkness into light, and that his cup will again run over with happiness. He refuses to doubt that goodness and mercy will pursue him all the days of his life! (Ps 23:1-6).

However, there *is* tension in the Psalm. His bold anticipation of *"goodness and mercy"* could not prevent trouble from coming upon him. He was unable to walk around the chilly shadows of death, but had to pass through that dark valley. He knew better than to demand unalloyed prosperity; he understood that pain and perplexity were also part of life.

So there is a balance to be maintained: on the one hand, we too must recognise that *"we are born to trouble as surely as sparks rise upward"* (Jb 5:7); but on the other, we should set ourselves, like true optimists, to expect only the best the Father can give. By so doing we make ourselves ready to cope equally well with either prosperity or adversity.

Few people seem able to do that. Either they are too elated by success, or too shattered by defeat, which keeps them plunging up and down as if they were riding some unpredictable big dipper.

Some Christians, thinking that true piety demands self-abnegation and poverty, cannot bear to be given prosperity. Others, convinced that true faith must bring unbroken joy and growing riches, are devastated when adversity strikes them. Both opinions distort scripture.

Faith certainly expects bountiful blessing, but also knows how to cope with disappointment; it reaches out for miracles, but knows how to encompass hardship. That is the true equilibrium of faith, and people who have achieved such balance are unlikely to suffer depression.

## WE ARE ALL DIFFERENT

> *My child, keep on examining yourself for as long as you live. Note what is bad for you, and stay away from it! Everything is not good for everyone; we do not all enjoy the same things. So do not be greedy for every delicacy, nor seek every pleasure without restraint (Sirach 37:27-29).*

Part of learning how to handle fluctuating fortune calmly lies in recognising how different we are from each other. Ask God for wisdom to know what does and what does not belong to you. Some things that are good for your neighbour may be bad for you. As an old English proverb says: *"All meat is not the same in every man's mouth;"* and again, *"One man's meat is another's poison."* So do not commit the folly of either envying what another has, nor of scorning him for what he lacks.

Contented people, well-balanced, living joyfully in fellowship with God, have learned to be happy with the shape divine providence has given their lives. If a chance comes along to reach for better things, they willingly seize it. If not, they rest serene in the knowledge that their times are in God's hands (Ps 31:15).

Paul once told some slaves that they should cast off their shackles only if a lawful opportunity arose to do so, for there was no disgrace in being a slave (1 Co 7:21). They were still children of the King, and could still gain the highest status in heaven! In fact, some translators think the passage should read: *"Even if you can gain your freedom, you should prefer to stay as you are, and make the most out of your present situation."* In any case, Paul's basic position is clear enough: neither master nor owner has any advantage at the throne of God. In their different ways, both groups can serve God equally well.

The apostle himself had learned the secret of staying contented, whether he had much or little (Ph 4:11-12). He insisted that he could *"face anything in the strength of Christ!"* (vs. 13).

Notice too how readily Paul acknowledges the different capacity of people to exercise control over themselves (1 Co 7:36-38). Because a time of persecution was about to ravage the church at Corinth, Paul thought that single people should remain unmarried. But he did not insist on it. He understood that while some couples may find celibacy an easy discipline, for others it is impossible. In the end, he advised them all to do what their individual temperaments required.

Plainly then, we are free to take advantage of whatever opportunities lie before us, but should not fret if the doors remain firmly closed. Nor should we feel that whatever someone else has we deserve too, nor that they ought to have all that we have. Rather, let us accept graciously and cheerfully, without either boasting or envy, who we are, what we have, and where we are placed.

If you do this, your life will be fragrant with the beauty of Christ.

---

**POINTS TO PONDER**

➤ "No one can handle prosperity safely unless he is also ready to cope serenely with adversity." Does that seem to you to be a wise saying? Or should we Christians set ourselves to expect and receive from God only prosperity?

➤ Find some other passages in scripture like *Psalm 23,* which balance an expectation from the hand of God of endless *"goodness and mercy"* against the reality of human pain.

➤ The version of the *Lord's Prayer* quoted above contains the clause, *"lead us not into temptation."* It seems a strange request. Does God ever lead his people toward temptation? What then does it mean? Check it out in as many commentaries as you can.

➤ Is it conceivable that Paul actually *did* advise slaves not to grab for freedom, even when it was offered to them?

CHAPTER TEN:

# FAITH UNDER FIRE

You can stretch only so high; you can lift only so much. If you try to carry more than your strength will bear, you may do yourself great harm; if you try to reach beyond your grasp you will probably fall over.

Five hundred years before Jesus was born, a Greek slave and story-teller strove to impress this wisdom upon his hearers –

## "THE EAGLE AND THE JACKDAW"

*An Eagle, swooping down on powerful wings, seized a lamb in her talons and made off with it to her nest. A Jackdaw saw the deed and his silly head was filled with the idea that he was big and strong enough to do as the Eagle had done. So with much rustling of feathers and a fierce air, he came down swiftly on the back of a large Ram. But when he tried to rise again he found that he could not get away, for his claws were tangled in the wool. And so far was he from carrying away the Ram, that the Ram hardly noticed he was there.*

*The Shepherd saw the fluttering Jackdaw and at once guessed what had happened. Running up, he caught the bird and clipped its wings. That evening he gave the Jackdaw to his children.*

*"What a funny bird this is!" they said, laughing. "What do you call it, father?"*

*"That is a Jackdaw, my children. But if you should ask him, he would say that he is an Eagle!"*

*Moral: Do not let your vanity make you overestimate your powers.* [38]

The moral from that fable has been reiterated by countless sages across the centuries, not least among them our old friend the rabbi—

> *Sensible people do not meddle in affairs that are too hard for them. Nor do they keep on asking about things they are not meant to know. . . . Nor do they interfere in matters that are not their business. They know that they can hardly handle properly even the things that have been given to them!*
>
> *So be humble enough to admit that there are some things you don't know; cast aside reluctance to admit your errors. Only a fool tries to stop the tide from coming in. Why would you try to lift a weight that is too heavy for you?*
>
> *My son, do not get busy with too many things; if you try to do too much you will find yourself at fault. Chase as hard as you please, still you will not catch all of your prey. Flee as swiftly as you can, still the pursuer will catch you sometimes. . . . Good fortune and bad, life and death, poverty and riches – they all come from God." (Sirach 3:21-24; 13:2; 4:26; 11:10-14).*

At sixteen years of age, I could pick up a bag of superphosphate [39] toss it over my shoulder, walk off with it, empty it into a spreader, go back for another, and keep it up all day. Today, nearly 50 years later, I doubt if I could even drag such a weight along the ground. And having no wish to cripple myself, I certainly would not try to

---

[38]  The Aesop for Children, Rand McNally & Co., Chicago; 1984 edition; pg. 12.

[39]  Which then weighed (I think) 187 pounds, or about 85 kilograms.

pick it up. But there are things I *can* do now, which as a young man I would never have dared to attempt. So each day brings its own weakness, and its own strength. Lift what you can, and leave the rest alone! Do what is proper for you, and don't meddle where you don't belong! Too many people, including pastors, fall into a fault because they get too busy doing too many things.

Have you noticed in the gospels how narrow was the focus of Jesus' life and ministry. He was adamant that he had come to do only the Father's will – nothing more; nothing less. He walked past scores of desperately hurting people, making no attempt to comfort or heal them (see, for example, John 5:1-9, where he selected only one man from among a *"multitude"* of diseased and crippled people). Indeed, the world has always been vastly more scandalised by what Jesus did *not* do than by what he *did*. Here is what one renowned atheist had to say about Jesus of Nazareth –

> *I now want to say a few words upon . . . the question whether Christ was the best and wisest of men. It is generally taken for granted that we shall agree that that was so. I do not myself. . . I do not believe that one can grant either the superlative wisdom or the superlative goodness of Christ as depicted in the Gospels.* [40]

He then lists various places in the gospels where the words and actions of Christ violate the normal canons of social behaviour. Jesus spoke not one word of protest about the Roman occupation of Palestine, nor did he denounce the torture chambers and child brothels that existed in every major city. Slaves sobbing under the harsh tyranny of their oppressors found no champion in Christ. He

---

[40] Lord Bertrand Russell, Why I Am Not A Christian; Unwin Books, London, 1975; pg. 20-22.

paid the Roman taxes without complaint, and gave no countenance to any kind of political revolution.

Even when he was offered two chances to seize the reins of government he scorned them (Mt 4:8; 21:8-9).

His kingdom was not of this world, and he declined to become involved in trying to solve its political and social problems.

I do not mean that he did not care about human misery. Was he not the man who wept when he visited Jerusalem and found the city stricken and oppressed? (Lu 13:34). Was he not moved with deepest pity when he saw the crowds, for *"they were like sheep without a shepherd, harassed and helpless"?* (Mt 10:36).

Nonetheless, Jesus knew what he had come to do, and he permitted nothing to turn him aside from that purpose. He understood how mistaken it would be to allow himself to be dominated by

## THE DEMANDS OF THE URGENT

Don't be controlled by the important, the urgent, or even the necessary, but only by the Father's will. You cannot solve every person's problems, you cannot meet every person's need, nor should you try to do so. Jesus refused to be pressured into stepping outside his proper role, even when he was confronted by manifest injustice, or even when it lay within his power to right a wrong *(see Luke 12:13-15).* He refused to dissipate his energy by scattering good deeds far and wide. He understood not only what was desirable, but better, what was achievable. What he *could* do, within the Father's purpose, he did; what was outside that purpose, or unachievable, he avoided.

## ATTEMPTING TOO MUCH

Christians are sometimes grandiose in their expectations. For example, in a sermon recently I heard a preacher boldly proclaim that "the church controls the destiny of the nation!" Now that may be true in some kind of narrow and limited sense, but in general it is false. Worse, it places an intolerable burden upon the church. We are not ultimately responsible for the wellbeing and prosperity of the nation. How can we be, when scripture says that the land lies in the grip of the Evil One, who can do with it largely as he pleases? *(See Luke 4:5-6; 1 John 5:19)*.

The history of the early church is a telling demonstration of this, for one of the most awful problems that faced 3rd-century Christians was a seeming paradox. Just about the time that more than half of the population had become Christian the empire began to reel under a series of terrifying invasions. After a bitter struggle the foreigners were driven out, but many pagans complained, with some justice, that so long as Rome had worshipped her traditional gods, the empire had waxed mighty, but now that the Christians were prevailing the empire was stricken with woe!

## A CHRISTIAN NATION DESTROYED

By the end of the 4th century the whole empire had become at least nominally Christian. Yet hardly more than a century later, with the church supreme from west to east, the empire was torn to shreds by the invading Huns, Goths, Vandals, and others. Only its eastern half survived the debacle. In the west, rape and pillage, desolation and ruin, spread everywhere.

Where was the God of the Christians? Why had he not protected the lands, possessions, and lives of his own people? How could the empire have been stronger and more prosperous when it worshipped pagan deities than after it had turned to Christ?

The answer, of course, lies in Jesus' own words. The church is called to be *"the salt of the earth"*, but not the earth itself. We are *"the leaven in the lump"*, we are not the dough. We are *"the light on the hill"*, but not the hill. Our task is not to rule the nation, but to die for it; we are not its masters, but its servants. Nor do we have any promised control, nor even substantial influence, over its destiny. How much the church can affect the future of the land depends more on factors that are out of our control than it does upon any unilateral decision we Christians might make.

I am speaking about the church, not about individual Christians. By all means let qualified men and women seek office at all levels of government; let us all, as individuals, do whatever we can to ameliorate the lot of our neighbours and to improve the happiness of our community. But it is not the duty of the *church* to conquer the nation for Christ. We have no command to do that, nor any guarantee of success should we attempt it. We should instead focus upon the task God has plainly given us: plant churches and make disciples, as many as we can while it is still *"day"* and before *"the night comes when no one will be able to work"* (Jn 9:4).

## WORLD EVANGELISATION?

Similarly, I was once asked by a group of ministers to answer the question, "What is God's programme for world evangelisation?" I had to say that I didn't think God had any such plan, and that in any case it was not our problem. The *Great Commission* is clear enough: *"Go out into all nations, preach the gospel, and make disciples"* (Matthew 28:19; Mark 16:15). Nothing there about conquering the earth. We have no obligation to be statistically successful evangelists, but only faithful *witnesses* (Ac 1:8, Greek, *martus = witness* or *martyr*, 22:20). That witness may lead to a vast harvest of souls; it may just as well lead to imprisonment, torture, and death.

But now, coming back to our starting point, and to the more ordinary matter of how we live each day, here is the lesson to learn: *it is wiser to do one thing well than a dozen things poorly.* It is also more conducive to happiness and less productive of depression.

So separate yourself from that company of driven men and women who are frantically busy day and night, ever trying to achieve more and more, never satisfied, always haunted by a sense of failure. They are prime candidates for stomach ulcers and nervous breakdowns. They do not exemplify the way of the Lord.

The way of Christ is calm and untroubled. Even if a storm is raging around you, where Jesus is there should be an epicentre of peace –

- ➤ what he has given you to do you can do with trustful confidence
- ➤ within the resources that he has made available
- ➤ using the strength that he provides
- ➤ calling on the wisdom that he freely gives (Ja 1:5-8).

Anything else is of the earth, and **stands** outside the kingdom of God.

## POINTS TO PONDER

➤ In what ways do many people (including Christian pastors) harm themselves by reaching for things that are simply beyond their grasp?

➤ Think about Lord Russell's indictment of Jesus as a man he could not admire. How would Jesus behave today? What issues would he address? What protests would he raise? Or would he do just as he did before?

➤ It has been said, "the church controls the destiny of the nation." Why is that statement foolish and far removed from the truth?

➤ What answer would *you* give to someone who asks you, "What is God's programme for world evangelisation?"

## CHAPTER ELEVEN:

# FAITH UNDER FIRE

One of the more painful discoveries of Christian life is that answers to prayer may be long delayed. How easy it is then to plunge into despair, to think that God has abandoned his child, to feel that nothing remains except misery – see Psalm 31:9-13.

Will you then throw away your faith?

The psalmist was made of sterner stuff. On the very edge of the abyss he pulled back, renewed his faith, and cried –

> *But in you Lord I will put all my trust. This is what I will say: "You are my God and my times are in your hand . . . Let your face shine upon me, for I am your servant. In your unchanging love save me from all my foes (vs.14-16).*

This idea of delayed answers to prayer occurs in many places in scripture, which says that by waiting we are taught patience and faith is toughened.

In one place the apostle addresses a group of Christians who had shown remarkable fortitude under persecution. They had not only endured suffering without complaint, they went further and accepted privation *"cheerfully"* (He 10:34). But now, because their troubles had been prolonged, they seemed in danger of giving up hope and of yielding to doleful pessimism. So he begged them –

> *Do not throw away your confidence, for nothing else can bring such a great reward. Yes, you will need patience. But if you keep on doing God's will you cannot fail to gain all that he has promised. For what does the scripture say? "In just a little while he who has promised to come will come; he will not delay!" (vs. 35-37).*

Do you notice the startling tension in that passage? On the one hand the apostle is emphatic: Christ will come to them very soon, he will not delay, they will shortly receive every promised blessing.

But he is just as insistent that on the other hand they must be patient. But why do they need patience if God is going to answer their prayers *"very soon"*? Surely the idea of *"patience"* presupposes a long delay? Surely the promise of *"soon"* removes the need for patience?

## A STATE OF TENSION

But that kind of tension can be found throughout the Bible. Much depends upon whether you are looking at an event through the eyes of heaven or of earth. As Peter said,

> *Here is something, beloved, you should never forget: to the Lord one day may be like a thousand years, and a thousand years like one day. So he is not, as some of you have supposed, tardy in fulfilling his promise, but rather he is patient with you. He does not want anyone to be lost, but strives to bring everyone to repentance (2 Pe 3:8-9).*

Against that background, the unknown author of *Hebrews* urges his readers not to make the terrible mistake of backsliding. There is only one sensible thing for them to do. No matter how long God delays his answers, they must abide by this rule –

> *My righteous servant (says the Lord) must live only by faith; if anyone shrinks back, my soul will no longer delight in him (10:38).*

But surely you, dear reader, are not among those who lack the heart to press on? Will you fall back and lose everything? Never! Rather let us together stir up faith, and go forward, determined to grasp the uttermost salvation of our God (verse 39).

## POINTS TO PONDER

➢ Sometimes a delayed answer to prayer may be nothing more than that: a delay. An affirmative answer is eventually assured. Other times, delay may in fact mean *"No!"* How can you tell the difference? How should delay be handled?

➢ Many parts of the Bible exist in tension with other parts – for example, how does human freedom of choice relate to divine sovereignty? Can you think of other places where this tension is found?

➢ Have there been times in the past when you have given up too soon, only to realise later that if you had persevered you would have known victory instead of defeat?

CHAPTER TWELVE:

*CHAPTER TWELVE:*

# ACCEPTING YOURSELF

Some people are too much aware that their problems are self-caused. No doubt their assessment is correct, for are we not all our own worst enemy? Nonetheless, it is a mistake to become so conscious of personal shortcomings that we despair of ever being able to change.

Equally, it is a mistake to suppose that anyone can change beyond a certain point – and that is the particular problem I want to take up here.

## WE ARE A "PACKAGE DEAL"

Merchants frequently offer "package deals", where shoppers can obtain certain goods at an excellent price, but only if they buy the package complete. Sometimes the merchant may refuse altogether to sell the separate parts. The shopper must buy all, or nothing.

We are like that – each one of us is a "package deal", a complete entity. We cannot be broken up into component pieces, saying of each piece, this part is excellent, this not so good, and this one quite worthless. It is all or nothing. No part can be removed or significantly altered without changing the entire package.

When a man courts a lady he would hardly dare offer to wed just one part of her, while discarding the rest. He must take the whole woman, the best with the worst, or no woman at all. Neither of the two wooers can indulge themselves in a bout of picking and choosing. They must love and accept each other as they are, or abandon the enterprise altogether.

We human beings are not just an amalgam of *virtues*, but also of *vices*, which are all entwined together, our strengths with our weaknesses. No doubt we should do what we can to build up whatever is good, and to diminish, even suppress, whatever is inadequate or faulty. But in the end, we cannot have one without the other. Any attempt to tear either part away would destroy us.

That is why no one ever really changes. Extroverts, even after conversion to Christ, tend to remain extroverts, and introverts do not suddenly become brazen. The new birth alters some aspects of a person's *behaviour*, refining and ennobling it, but it does not turn the convert into a wholly new *person*. Temperament, personality, the things that comprise a person's unique identity, his or her real self, may have some rough edges smoothed away, but essentially the person remains the same.

## GOD MADE NIGHT AND DAY

Consider nature. Every dawn must have its sunset, for day and night belong together. Neither can there be *up* without *down*, nor *in* except there is *out*, nor *left* unless there is *right*, nor *top* without *bottom*. Each thing is known finally only by its opposite. Thus we can hold to an idea of *brightness*, – that is, a sense of what it truly means – only as we also know *darkness*. Without the one we could have no way either of defining or even recognising the other.

Can a zebra have white stripes unless it also has black ones? Even a monarch must have two thrones, one lofty and splendid, the other small and lowly! Without possession of both seats, he cannot be king. It is a metaphor of life, for we are all a mixture of the noble and the ignoble. Like nature, we possess mountain peaks that cannot exist without their valleys, and valleys that would vanish without their mountains. Indeed it becomes a question, which depends upon which? Does the mountain make the valley, or the valley the mountain? At least this is known: take one of those words out of the dictionary and you will also have to take out the other! They belong inseparably together.

In the world of physics nearly everything depends upon sustaining a state of tension between two opposites. Thus an electric current results from a tension between negative and positive charges. No magnet can exist without two polarities, north and south. If the wind blows *toward* one place it must blow *away* from another. There is no outgoing tide without its incoming counterpart. Summer and winter, springtime and autumn, are indissolubly linked.

## "THE DARK SIDE OF THE FORCE"

All this, of course, has its origin in God, who declares about himself –

> *I alone am the Lord, and there is no other Maker. I make the light, and I make the darkness. I make pleasure and I make pain. I am the Lord, and I alone can do all these things. (Is 45:6b-7)* [41]

What does that mean? Simply that nothing in the world can exist unless it was first conceived in the mind of God. There is only one Creator, and there can be no other. Even the devil can use only what God first invented, and we too can never do any more than think God's thoughts after him. I do not mean that God deliberately planned every kind of iniquity, or that sin arises from some specific fiat of God. I mean only that in the very act of creating righteousness the Father inescapably called into being a *potential* for unrighteousness. He could not create the one without the other.

---

[41] Commenting on the mystery of how a righteous God can be called the author of both good and evil (Is 45:7), Keil & Delitzsh write: "The declaration is (very) bold . . . (but the) meaning of the words is not exhausted by those who content themselves with the assertion that by the 'evil' (or 'darkness') we are not to understand the evil of guilt, but the evil of punishment. Undoubtedly, evil as an act is not the direct working of God, but the spontaneous work of a creature endowed with freedom. At the same time, evil, as well as good, has in this sense its origin in God – that he combines within himself the first principles of love and wrath, the possibility of evil, the self-punishment of evil, and therefore the consciousness of guilt as well as the evil of punishment in the broadest sense." (Old Testament Commentary, in loc.)

When he conceived kindness he also had to make cruelty a possibility. When he endowed his creatures with love he also had to give them a capacity for hate. No sin is entirely the result either of satanic or human invention; no act of human barbarity has ever caught God by surprise, as something he never expected nor even imagined was possible. He has been aware from the very beginning of all possibilities, of all the darkness that is hidden behind the light.

Here is the true nature of the conflict between God and Satan: the devil yearns to reverse the precedence of light over darkness. The darkness (whether physical or moral) certainly has its origin in God, just as surely as the light springs from him – for there can be no light without darkness. But it was his decree that the darkness should always be hidden and that only the light should be known. Satan's intent has been to overturn God's decree, and to make darkness supreme. That is why he is called the *Prince of Darkness*. The devil did not create darkness (only God can create), but he has tried to misuse it. [42]

The makers of the *Star Wars* films, whether knowingly or not, reproduced this divine reality. They could not dream up a "force" without giving it both a good and a dark side, and then planting each of them in Darth Vader and in his son Luke Skywalker. Vader allowed the dark side to prevail, yet could not entirely rid himself of the good side; nor could Skywalker, who embraced the good side, entirely rid himself of its dark counterpart. The issue was not one of eradicating one side or the other, but only, which will dominate?

---

[42] Notice how God made the darkness first (Ge 1:2), and only afterwards the light, which Satan has ever since been trying to reverse.

# "ALL THINGS BRIGHT AND BEAUTIFUL"

Cecil Frances Alexander in 1848 wrote the song

> All things bright and beautiful,
> All creatures great and small,
> All things wise and wonderful,
> The Lord God made them all.

Although Mrs Alexander did include in her lines the words "*all* creatures great and small", it is hard to escape the impression that she had in mind only things "bright and beautiful". Her poem lacks any mention of the harsh realities of the natural world: the tiger's fang, the serpent's tooth, the scorpion's sting, sweet blossoms that kill, and all the other terrors that caused another poet to write –

> . . . Nature, red in tooth and claw
> With ravine, shriek'd against his creed. [43]

But the dark and the ugly are just as much God's creation as the bright and the beautiful. This is all a deep mystery, and no one yet has fully measured it.

In any case, I want to affirm here only that we are made in the image of God, from whom (scripture says) came both light and dark. Hence the same must be true of us: that is, we possess both a dark side and a good side, and must choose which will rule our lives.

In the world of morals, this means there can be no *righteousness* without at least a potential for *unrighteousness*. If I cannot recognise evil, then neither can I understand good, for those moral

---

[43] The "creed" is the belief that "God is love indeed, /And love Creation's final law." The pitiless savagery of the earth's carnivores seems to give the lie to this. "Ravine" here means to prey on something violently. Alfred Tennyson, In Memorium, sec. 56, st. 4.

opposites exist only in contrast with each other. No virtue can reside in me unless I also have some impulse toward, or latent talent for, vice. If a person is incapable of doing anything except what is good, then he can no longer be called "good" – his "virtue" is no more than his natural state of existence, morally neutral, unrecognisable as virtuous, and therefore undeserving of praise. That is why, in scripture, righteousness is always a dynamic thing and never merely an absence of evil. Rather, it is the result of choices made *despite* the presence of evil. Righteousness is active, positive, deliberate, shining brightly in contrast with the surrounding darkness.

Because of this principle of opposites, I know that no strength can exist in me unless I possess also the seed of its corresponding weakness. Every path has two sides, left and right. If one is removed, then it is no longer a path, just an open expanse. The dawn is made beautiful by the darkness that precedes it. I know that I am alive only because I have grasped the reality of death. So we are all an amalgam of two polarities, positive and negative.

What should we learn from this? Simply –

## ACCEPT YOURSELF AS YOU ARE

Do I mean that you may sin with impunity, or that you should care nothing about sin? Of course not. It may be true that there can be no righteousness apart from a potential for unrighteousness, but that is no reason to allow the "dark force" any ascendancy. Rather, we should be like Jesus who *"loved righteousness and hated iniquity"*.

But you do need also to recognise that every good trait you possess will have some kind of corresponding fault hovering in the shadows. If you want to display the finer side of your personality, you will have to deal patiently with its bad opposite.

For example, to write the forty or so books that have struggled out of my pen, I have had to spend thousands of hours alone in my study, with only my library for a companion. Such a life would have been unendurable if I had lacked the cargo of virtues needed by a writer, such as patience, assiduous study, self-discipline, skill with words, and the like. But that cargo also includes some inescapable negatives, such as a tendency to be introverted, to lack empathetic gifts, to be more focussed on ideas than on people, and the like. Now I am no slave to those negatives, and I have gone a long way toward diminishing their effects. But I cannot hope to rid myself altogether of them. To do so would make me another man, unable to complete the task that has been set for me.

## TREASURE IN A CLAY POT

Notice how Paul says that while God has given us many treasures (our virtues and graces), they are nonetheless confined within an *"earthen vessel"* (2 Co 4:7). You and I *are* a mixture of heaven and earth, flesh and spirit, intellect and emotion, wisdom and ignorance. You are probably strong where your neighbour is weak, yet for that very reason you may be weak where your neighbour is strong! That is why Paul urges each of us to think soberly about ourselves, not to assess ourselves either too high or too low, but to be honest (see *Romans 12:3-6*). So also, two centuries earlier, Sirach urged –

> *Never be ashamed simply to be yourself. You can be so self-effacing that it becomes a sin, whereas there is another kind of modesty that will lead to honour and privilege. Some people out of respect for others are untrue to themselves, and they cause their own downfall by their misgivings. . . . It is good to be humble, but not at the cost of your self-respect. Evaluate yourself honestly, for who will honour you if you insist upon dishonouring yourself? If you keep on tearing yourself down, who will build you up? (4:20-22; 10:28-29).*

In another of his songs, Sir Thomas Wyatt echoed the same theme. That is, since you cannot change your innate character (any more than an Ethiopian his skin or a leopard his spots, Je 13:23), you might as well accept yourself as you are and get on with the job of living and of serving God –

> I am as I am and so will I be,
> But how that I am none knoweth truly.
> Be it evil, be it well, be I bond, be I free,
> I am as I am and so will I be.
> Who judgeth well, well God him send;
> Who judgeth evil, God them amend;
> To judge the best therefore intend,
> For I am as I am and so will I end.
> And from this mind I will not flee,
> But to you all who misjudge me
> I do protest, as ye may see,
> That I am as I am and so will be.

## PLEASANT DRESS

"Clothes make the man!" That is an old Dutch proverb, and the English have one like it: "Good clothes open all doors." The idea is this: the way a person dresses shows the quality of his or her self-respect. Untidy, unkempt dress reflects a slovenly internal image. But dressing well, making one's outward appearance as pleasant as possible, shows a quality of inner grace. Nice clothes can also bring a ray of sunshine into the gloomiest day! They can lift the most despondent spirit!

That rule, of course, is far from absolute. Some of the nastiest people in the world have been superbly dressed, and some of the best have worn rags. Nonetheless, it is generally true that garments say a lot about the people who wear them –

> *You can tell what people are like just by the way they look. When you meet them face to face, you may quickly know whether or not they have good sense. Observe how they are dressed, the way they laugh, how they carry themselves – such things will*

*tell you something about their inner character*
*(Sirach 19:29-30).*

## GOOD MANNERS

Jesus dressed well, and conducted himself courteously. He wore a seamless robe that was too valuable for the careless soldiers to tear apart (Jn 19:23-24*).* And, following the Saviour's example, Peter enjoined courtesy upon the church: *"love each other like brothers, and always be gracious and courteous"* (1 Pe 3:8).

The ancient Greeks had a classic description for a true gentleman; they said that he must have a "good and honest heart." Would you be surprised to find that Jesus once applied those very words to the best of Christian believers? (see Lu 8:15). He understood that the kingdom of God could not be built upon a foundation of crudeness and incivility.

Good manners are acceptable anywhere, at all levels of society, and they add pleasantness to life. More importantly, they are enjoined in scripture –

> *In the fear of God, you must never be contemptuous of the deaf, nor deliberately cause a blind person to stumble. I am the Lord. . . . If an elderly person comes into the room, rise to your feet; always be respectful to those who are older than you. Do these things in the fear of your God. I am the Lord. (Le 19:14,32).*

One cannot help but be struck by the solemn backdrop against which Moses placed those injunctions. The setting seems too heavy for the contents, like putting a massive gilt frame around a small and unimportant sketch. Twice he said, *"in the fear of your God"*, and twice he cited divine authority, *"I am the Lord."*

What else can it mean except this? – The Lord God treats good manners seriously; they are an important part of godly behaviour. If anyone claims to fear God and to acknowledge him as Lord, then let that person display courteous and gracious conduct toward all people. See also

> ➤ Ge 31:35; Sir 4:7-10, 29-30; 6:5; 8:3,6-7; 9:18; 11:8; 19:7-10; 20:5-8; 21:20-26; 23:13-15; 25:20; 26:14-16,24-27; 27:12-15; 31:12-20; 32:1-11; 41:19-42:1 (*"don't put your elbows on the table at mealtime"*); 2 Es 2:20-22; [44] Pr 23:1-2

> ➤ notice the politeness of Eliphaz ;in Jb 4:2 (plus 3,4); 29:8; 32:6-7; etc.

> ➤ William of Wykeham (1324-1404) [45] coined the saying: "Manners maketh man", which sentiment was echoed by the German poet-philosopher Goethe (1749-1832) in his *Proverbs in Prose* –

A man's manners are a mirror in which he shows his portrait.

The question is: what portrait are you and I showing to the world?

## TREATING ANIMALS WELL

The biblical idea of a gracious, courteous, and gentle life-style, is strengthened by various injunctions to show kindness to animals –

> *. . . on the seventh day you must not do any work, neither you . . . nor your ox, your donkey, nor any of your animals . . . so that they may rest as you do. . .*

---

[44] This passage is actually a piece of Christian writing. It was added to 2 *Esdras* by an unknown editor, probably around the year 100 A.D. Its Christian intention and origin is shown by vs. 10-13. It shows that courteous behaviour and care of the needy were major concerns of the early church.

[45] English churchman and statesman, he founded New College in Oxford, and also the Winchester School. He had an enormous influence upon the development of education in England.

*. You must not muzzle an ox while it is treading out the grain (De 5:14; 25:4).*

*Good people care about their animals, but those who are cruel are wicked at heart . . . Suppose you come across the donkey of someone who hates you, fallen under a heavy burden? No matter how reluctant you are, you must help the animal to get back on its feet (Pr 12:10; Ex 23:5).*

*You must not boil a kid in its mother's milk. . . . You must not yoke an ox and a donkey together to your plough (Ex 23:19; 34:26; De 14:21; 22:6,10).*

*O Lord, you are alike concerned about both people and animals (Ps 36:6b).*

A thousand years later Sirach quoted Moses –

There is a happy farmer: one who does not yoke an ox and an ass together to his plough (25:8; see also 22:32).

Indeed, there are more than a score of places in Sirach's book of wisdom where the old rabbi urges courteous, mannerly, and gentle behaviour upon his readers. He knows that this is a prescription for living harmoniously with one's world, at peace with the creation, being able to enjoy all the beauty that God has placed on this earth of ours, godly people will take those rules seriously, and live by them. Nor will they lose anything by it. On the contrary, such behaviour will make them more pleasant to others, more delightful to God, and life will be more congenial to them. It is, as they say in the classics, a "win-win" situation.

These ideas are developed further in the next chapter.

## POINTS TO PONDER

➤ Scripture describes us as God's *"new creation"*. How then can it be said that conversion to Christ does not turn the Christian into "a wholly new person"?

➤ In *Isaiah*, God says, *"I make the light and I make the darkness."* Those words apply to both the natural and the moral world. Think about their inevitability. In other words, how can God make *light* unless he also makes *darkness*?

➤ Sin ultimately has its origin in God; but only in the sense that God could not conceive virtue without at the same time creating at least a *potential* for vice. In God himself there is not the smallest shadow (Ja 1:17).

➤ Reckon up your own strengths, and then face honestly their weakening counterparts in your character. How should you handle this amalgam of the desirable and the undesirable?

➤ Can a person truly display the character of Christ, or reflect the dynamics of the kingdom of God, apart from worthy manners and acceptable dress?

## CHAPTER THIRTEEN:

# NICE PEOPLE, NICE MANNERS

They are nice people, with nice manners,
But got no money at all! [46]

Such depression comes from ignoring what the Bible says about the way we should relate to each other. We are told to be patient, tolerant, generous, kind, gentle, longsuffering, and the like, not harsh, nor vindictive, nor resentful, nor unforgiving.

It would seem easy enough to obey those instructions. They don't require riches or scholarship, just common sense. Why then do so many people make such hard going out of their relationships?

Here is one reason: they make the double mistake of either expecting too much from each other, or too little. If you demand too much from people, you may crush them; if you demand too little, you may humiliate them. Furthermore, when they fail to meet your expectations, you may find yourself trapped in a prison of disappointment, hurt, and frustration.

Most people, I suppose, are likely to be guilty of setting their demands too high rather than too low. Our fallen nature is motivated by a larger instinct to grab than to give. But no one can *extract* happiness out of another person. Happiness comes from others only when they offer it as a gift, in response to your bestowal of happiness upon them.

---

[46] Words from a popular song of the 1940s.

Paul summed it up by saying that we should *"walk worthy of Christ"*, and he urged upon the church three great qualities (Ep 4:1-2) –

# HUMILITY

The Greek word seems to have been coined by the church, for there is no evidence in any other literature of its prior use. The early Christians brought together two other words, *lowly* and *mind*, and created a new word to describe the grace of *humility*. The idea is one of having a modest and humble opinion of oneself, not puffed-up, not arrogant.

Why did they need a new word? Because humility was a despised quality in the ancient world, and the culture had no positive word to describe it. To the Greeks and Romans, humility was associated with a cowering slave; it suggested a cringing and timid person, ignoble, and mean. Even today, in the secular world, that is probably still how most people view humility. The adulation of the masses is usually devoted to highly successful, ambitious, ruthless, aggressive heroes. We are prone to admire more, not those who yearn to serve us, but those who crave to rule us.

## THE EXAMPLE OF JESUS

What a different pattern Jesus set, both in his actions and in his words! In one place he said –

> *Out there in the world, kings lord it over their subjects, and those who seize authority expect to be called 'Benefactors'! That is not how you should behave. Let the greatest among you reckon themselves the least, and let those who want to rule turn themselves into your servants (Lu 22:25-26).*

Jesus gave his most graphic demonstration of this rule when he did what no other religious leader before him had ever done: he took a little child and set it before the people as a model of how they should live (see Mt 18:1-3).

## LIKE A LITTLE CHILD

Even in our time that idea remains revolutionary. But in Bible days it was utterly shocking. Children were not admired then as they are now; they were not pictured as unspoiled and innocent. They were not seen as possessors of a charming naturalness, virgin and quaint. They were not held up as paragons of sweet and pure love. Those are largely 19th-century notions.

Until quite modern times the life of a child was cheap; children were reckoned weak and helpless, akin to beggars in their dependence upon the charity of others. No one thought it strange when they were made to work in the fields and factories. Thousands of children drudged every day in the workhouses and coalpits, treated hardly better than pack animals.

Jeremiah lamented that *"young men were toiling at the grinding mill, while boys staggered under loads of wood"* (La 5:13). But his main grief was that they were labouring for a foreign taskmaster. Had they been working for an Israelite he would have stayed silent. The Babylonians themselves probably saw nothing unduly oppressive in forcing children to toil so hard. Did not the same happen in far off Babylon?

The ancients never praised children nor said they had delightful graces that adults should emulate. They gave to their children about the same status as slaves, and treated them accordingly. Hence the punishment for both a rebellious child and a recalcitrant slave was the same –

> You should never be ashamed of frequently punishing your children, nor of drawing blood from the back of a stubborn slave. . . A man who loves his son will whip him often . . . for just as an unbroken horse runs wild, so an unbridled son will become unruly.

> If you pamper a child he will grieve you, if you play with him he will take advantage of you. Do you

want to share his pain? Then go and share his laughter! But if you dislike gnashing your teeth, then give your son no freedom in his youth.

Never excuse a boy's errors; crush stubbornness while he is still a child; beat him black and blue while he is still young. If you don't, he will grow up lawless and disobedient, and he will break your heart. So discipline your son, and put a slave's yoke on him. Then perhaps he will not shame you by some disgraceful act. (Sirach 42:1,5; 30:1,8-13).

In another place the rabbi insists that a son must "serve his parents as a slave does his master" (3:7), and he tells how livestock, slaves, wives, sons, daughters should be treated equally and dispassionately as a man's private property (7:22-26). See also 33:25-30, where the same whip prescribed for wayward sons is recommended for defiant slaves.

Now I am of course repelled by such brutality, and far removed from endorsing it. [47] But it does show us what Jesus meant when he told us to become like children. We are to be "humble" – lowly of mind, not domineering, nor proud; but vulnerable, small in our own eyes, owing a debt of love and of service both to God and to our neighbour.

## ALL HUMILITY

Notice how strongly Paul insists upon our conformity to this rule. He says, *"behave in a manner that is worthy of the high calling*

---

[47] One of the happy consequences of the gospel has been an elevation of the status of people who were formerly either belittled or considered fair prey for the strong: *women, children, servants,* and *strangers.* Paul's words, forbidding such exploitation, were revolutionary in their day (see for example, Colossians 3:18-4:6). It has taken a long time, but the full effect of those ideas is at last being seen in our day.

*you received, with <u>all</u> humility"* (Ep 4:1-2). He means, do not be humble only when it is convenient, but also when it is inconvenient; not only when you hope to get some benefit from it, but also when humility is to your disadvantage. *All* humility – at all times, in all circumstances, under all provocation, to display unwaveringly the mind of Christ.

Those who have embraced *"all* humility" will ever be more willing to give than to get, to serve than to rule, to sacrifice than to demand. They are aware of God's greatness and of their smallness. They do not give themselves airs. They know how ephemeral life is; they remember that they are under sentence of death, and after that comes the judgment.

*"The meek,"* said Jesus, are those who will finally *"inherit the earth"* (Mt 5:5). Not bullies. Not the strong. Even less those who turn away from God. But those who allow the meekness of Christ to shape their words and actions each day.

The second quality that Paul said should mark our relationships is

## GENTLENESS

Aristotle admired the Greek word translated "gentleness". He described it as the "golden mean"; for it expresses a virtue that is the midpoint between being too angry and never angry, and included the wisdom to know the difference.

Animal trainers in Bible days used the same word to describe an animal that had been properly tamed. They wanted the beast to keep its strength and spirit, but to be brought under command. An improperly trained animal, broken in spirit, listless, and terrified, was worthless. The creature had to be made obedient, yet lose nothing of its energy and zest for life.

When applied to Christian life, *"gentleness"* teaches us two things–

## 1) A GENTLE PERSON KNOWS WHEN TO BE ANGRY

Watch the furious Jesus with a whip in his hand throwing down the tables of the moneychangers and driving them out of the Temple (Mt 21:12-13). Listen to his fierce denunciation of some hypocritical religious leaders –

> *Woe to you, scribes and pharisees, you hypocrites! . . . You clean a cup or a plate on the outside, but leave the inside filthy, full of greed and self-indulgence. . . . You are like a beautifully kept cemetery, lovely on the outside, but inside full of dead bones and decay. . . . You snakes! You brood of vipers! How can you escape being condemned to hell? (Mt 23:13, 25, 27, 33).*

Anger in itself is not a sin. Indeed, there are times when it would be iniquitous _not_ to be angry. Cruelty to children, for instance, should arouse the fiercest wrath in even the gentlest heart. Against child-molesters, rapists, heretics who divide the church, liars, tyrants, and other assorted ravagers of human happiness our indignation should burn hot. One is entitled to be angry with a wilfully disobedient child, or against deliberate and avoidable stupidity by adults. And no doubt there are other circumstances where anger is an appropriate response – although it should always be controlled, and never more excessive than the circumstances require.

In general, then, we may say that anger against harm done to others is warranted; seldom however are we justified in getting angry about harm done to ourselves. So the second idea that springs out of the word "gentleness" is this:

## 2) A GENTLE PERSON KNOWS WHEN NOT TO BE ANGRY

A true Christian, says Paul, would rather _be_ wronged than _do_ wrong. For example, some of the people in the church at Corinth had entered into law suits against each other. The apostle was scandalised, and he cried –

> *If you must have quarrels with one another here is what I think you should do: find the person who has the lowest standing in the church, and let him be the judge between you! I say that to make you feel ashamed. . . . Don't you realise that the moment you go to law against a fellow Christian you have already been defeated?* **Why not let yourself be wronged? Why not let yourself be defrauded?** *Instead, you go about wronging and defrauding each other – the very people who are your brothers and sisters! (1 Co 6:1-8).*

By all means defend others; but be content to allow *God* to be *your* defence. Do you deserve to be defended? Then you can find no better advocate than the Lord. But if you or your rights are not worth defending, then it is foolish to arm yourself for battle. You will only find yourself fighting God –

> *Has someone done you harm? Do not curse them, but ask God to bless them – yes, to bless them! . . . Resist the urge to pay back evil for evil. Aim for something higher, something that others will call noble. As much as you possibly can, to the very limit of your ability, strive to live at peace with everybody.*
>
> *Never seek revenge. Instead, leave God room to act on your behalf. Has he not said, 'Vengeance is mine, and I will repay'. . . This is what you should do: if your enemy is hungry, give him a meal; if your enemy is thirsty, give him a drink. By doing this, you will heap burning coals onto his head! Never let yourself be overcome by evil; rather, let your goodness overcome evil (Ro 12:14-21).*

What a wonderful church we would have, and what true happiness would fill our lives, if all the saints diligently practised these things! The third rule of relationships is this –

## PATIENCE

The English word used in older versions of the Bible was *"longsuffering"* = "long and patient endurance of injuries, troubles, and insults." Sounds rather dreary! But only on the pages of a dictionary; in reality, there is no life so exciting, rewarding, or fulfilling.

Why do we need "patience"? Simply because none of us can escape having to face seemingly unbearable people and situations. How can we cope with them? Only by allowing the Holy Spirit to fill us with the love and patience of Christ. How else can we stop ourselves from striking back at those who wrong us? How else can we *"turn the other cheek"* or *"go a second mile"*? (Mt 5:39-42). Who among us, without God's help, is equal to the demand, *"Love your enemies, and pray for those who persecute you"* (vs. 44). How impossible Christ's rule seems: *"You must be perfect therefore, just as your heavenly Father is perfect"* (vs. 48).

Of course, he does not mean that we must attain a kind of absolute perfection in every respect. He is talking here about *love*. He means that we should place no limit upon our willingness to reach out to everyone around us in love. The thought should never be in my mind, "I will love this fellow so long as he does not hurt me anymore. But if he does, then let him look out for himself. I will strike him back harder than ever he struck me!"

An old Swahili proverb says, "Begin with patience and end with pleasure." To which the Russians added, "Patience will overcome everything." And the Irish, "Patience is a virtue that causes no shame." And the Japanese, "Patience is bitter, but its fruit is sweet." [48] It seems a hard furrow to plough, but in the end there is no sweeter way to cross the rough fields of life.

## A BESETTING SIN

If patience is so useful, what shall we say about impatience, which is one of the besetting sins of our day? The Chinese put it succinctly: "A little impatience spoils great plans." [49]

What harm people bring upon themselves, what sorrows they create, by impatience! They demand the right to immediate satisfaction, to clutch personal pleasure, to be denied no happiness. And they want it all _now_! They cannot bear the thought that someone might be enjoying a happiness they do not know, or a pleasure they may not discover until later, or may never find at all.

But happiness by itself is not a valid quest for a Christian. Our chief goal must be to pursue _holiness_, without which we cannot even see, let alone enter, the kingdom of God (He 12:14).

## A BRAVE BISHOP

I do not mean that you must abjure happiness, or even pleasure. That would be silly. Many pleasures are innocent enough, and quite permissible for Christians. Yet the fact remains that you or I may be not be able to try them all and still remain true to the purpose of God. What God permits _you_, he may not permit _me_. Some things that you are forbidden I am allowed. In the end our sole and lasting joy must be to do God's will.

> _Illustration: Babylas was bishop of Antioch in the early part of the 3rd. century. A profoundly godly_

---

[48]  Encyclopedia of World Proverbs, Wolfgang Mieder; Prentice-Hall Inc, New Jersey, 1986; selections # 12079, 12089, 12100, 12103.

[49]  Ibid. # 8326.

*man, he was also noted for dauntless courage. The emperor Philip the Arabian came to an Easter service in 244, but Babylas barred his entrance. He insisted that the emperor must first do penance for a murder he had committed.*

*Some six years later, Philip was dethroned and killed by Decius. Then, because the church had supported the Arabian, the new emperor launched against it the worst persecution it had yet suffered. Babylas was imprisoned, tortured mercilessly, and eventually martyred. Just before he died, he left instructions that nothing should be buried with him except his chains – the symbol of his loyalty to God.*

His disciples did as he asked. He was buried naked, without a coffin, and only his chains were placed in the grave with him. Perhaps on resurrection morning he will rise with them alone in his hand.

In any case, we could hardly set ourselves a better aim than this: to come to the end of our lives boasting only of the chains we have worn for Christ. What are they? For most of us they will not be made of iron. Instead, they will be the chains of love we have forged around our souls, the chains of humility and patience, the chains of faithful service and daily obedience. These are the loveliest ornaments. They alone remain imperishable in the grave.

## POINTS TO PONDER

➤ Under the impact of the late-18$^{th}$ century evangelical revivals, attitudes toward children began to change until by the mid-19$^{th}$ century laws were being passed throughout Europe, either banning or modifying child labour. What other social changes has the gospel brought about in our world?

➤ The world often equates *humility* with *servility*. What distinction does scripture make between those two traits?

➤ How can a gentle and humble person be active, creative, forceful, confident, and even, if required, furiously angry?

➤ In what sense can we fulfil the injunction to *"be perfect as your Father in heaven is perfect"*?

*CHAPTER FOURTEEN:*

# LIVING, LOVING, LAUGHING!

Three things are pleasant to see, for they delight the eyes of God and of other people: children playing happily together; friendship among neighbours; and a husband and wife who love each other (Sir 25:1)

What is the source of this beautiful harmony?

## THEY NOTICE EACH OTHER

A feeling of being neglected is the bane of many homes; as a wife once said, she would be happy if her husband would only give her the attention he gave to the family dog – a look, a word, and a touch! But then perhaps she should have greeted him in the same exuberant manner as the dog did!

A good time to start is early in the day, by saying "Good morning!" – with perhaps an added kiss! This is an excellent lesson to drill into children, especially when they are still young and malleable. I cannot help but think it insultingly rude when children or young people enter a room and fail to greet the adults who are there. Indeed, it is offensive to be ignored by *anybody*, young or old! The affront is even worse when they are family. Should a man ignore his wife, or a wife her husband, or children their parents, or even parents their children? Yet I have often seen it done, and been offended.

But that "dog" story does suggest the three main secrets to sustained love –

> *look!* – notice each other
> *talk!* – speak and listen to each other
> *touch!* – with love and compassion.

# THEY COMMUNICATE WITH EACH OTHER

Human relationships can suffer from either too little or too much communication –

## 1) TOO LITTLE

In a marriage, two different people are involved, with different views, desires, methods, and perceptions. Yet, in all matters of importance to their happiness, they must now become as one person in their goals, decisions, actions, and values.

This won't happen of its own accord. What then should a couple do?

> ➢ begin by discovering each other's "positions" on various matters, such as sex, children, money, duties, rights, ambitions, goals, hopes, and the like

> ➢ recognise those things that are too important for the other person to surrender or change, and graciously yield precedence in those areas

> ➢ be willing to compromise – you can't have it all your own way

> ➢ work toward a common mind on significant family issues, but allow each other much liberty in matters of personal preference (music, literature, hobbies, friends, etc.)

In doing these things, set your own pattern, conformable to your own family's needs, not bound by some outside rule, nor governed by the opinions or style of other people. There are always people around who think they know how to run your home better than you do! Listen to them with respect; but have the courage to do what is right for you, your spouse, and your children. In the end, you must work out between yourselves, and yourselves alone, how to run your home in the most congenial and effective way.

## 2) TOO MUCH

Beware of the urge to tell everything about everything! People are often moved to this folly by two misunderstood rules –

### a) "LIVE IN THE LIGHT"

*"Living in the light"* is undoubtedly a useful and biblical principle (cp. 1 Jn 1:5-7). But it needs to be tempered by common sense –

> *When people talk too much they keep digging pits for themselves to fall into. If you are sensible you will keep your mouth shut. (Pr 10:19)*

> *Those who are wise keep their thoughts hidden; but silly people open their mouths and ruin themselves. (10:14)*

> *If you are prudent, you will keep what you know to yourself, unlike those fools who cannot help blurting out whatever comes into their heads. (12:23)*

> *So you call yourself a person of discernment? Then you will keep a cool head and a close mouth! Even a fool, if he knows how to keep quiet, may be thought wise; so show good sense, and seal your lips! (17:27-28)*

> *Have you met people who must tell everything they know? There is more hope for a fool than there is for them. (29:20)*

> Have you learned a secret? Keep it to yourself; you will not burst! Don't be the kind of fool who suffers agony from a secret like a woman giving birth. A piece of news locked in the heart is more painful to him than an arrow through the leg. (Sir 19:10-12)

> Here is a man who maintains silence, and he is thought wise. Here is another who indulges in endless chatter, and he is loathed. (20:5)

and there are another two-score similar sayings in both Proverbs and Sirach, which can be summarised in the words –

*Silly people tell everything that is in their heads; but the prudent know when to keep their tongues still!*

Someone may protest, though, "Surely we should be totally honest with each other, and is not 'confession good for the soul'?" But not all sin, nor every fault, should to be told to another person. Some of it is better confessed only to God, especially if the main effect of your confession is to bring pain to an innocent party. Confession that hurts others while it eases the penitent is nothing but self-indulgence. So there are times when by far the best policy is to keep your counsel to yourself; or at least to share your secret only with someone who cannot be harmed by it.

Then a second rule that people often abuse is this –

### b) "BE RECONCILED TO EACH OTHER"

People often misconstrue one of the rules Jesus gave –

*Whenever you are making an offering at the altar, if you remember that someone has something against you, then at once turn around, leave your gift behind, and go and make peace with your brother or sister. Only then should you return and continue your offering (Mt 5:23-24).*

Notice carefully the circumstance: this rule comes into effect if *someone* has something against *me*, but not if *I* have something against *them*. If I am the offended one, then I must simply forgive the offender (as in Mk 11:25-26) –

*When you stand praying, <u>if you have anything against anyone</u>, then you must forgive that person, so that your Father in heaven may forgive all the wrong things that you have done. But if you refuse*

*to forgive others, then neither will your Father in
heaven forgive your wrongdoing.*

If I am the one who is upset, then it is nothing more than a piece of
self-indulgence for me to go and dump my grievance on whoever I
think has offended me. People who behave like that often enjoy a
self-righteous feeling of superiority. They may also be craving
some kind of subtle revenge. I do not mean that I am *never* free to
tell another person that his or her behaviour is wrong; but *before* I
approach those who have hurt me, I must be sure that I have
forgiven them *"from my heart"* (Mt 18:35). If there is bitterness,
malice, violence, pride, animosity, spite, reprisal in my heart
toward my neighbour, then, no matter what he or she has done to
me, *I* am the one at fault. I owe a debt of love to all, and scripture
insists that it must be paid!

## THEY AGREE ON PRIORITIES

Generally speaking, the proper order is –

- ➢ God
- ➢ Spouse
- ➢ Children
- ➢ Job
- ➢ Church.

That is, after placing God at the apex of my life, making him
supreme in all things, allowing *nothing* to exalt itself above him,
nor to take higher priority, then I may devote myself to my spouse.
Following her in order of commitment come children, then job,
then church. That is easy to say, but not so easy to do, because
worship and service of God is inseparably bound up with an active
involvement in the church. For this reason, people often allow
church activities to occupy too much of their time, to the
detriment, and sometimes the ruin, of their families. They excuse
their error by claiming that they *"must put God first"*.

Yes, God must stand first in all things, and sometimes that may
mean serving the church before anyone else. But remember that

scripture itself says that anyone who does not properly care for family members is *"worse than a heathen"*! (1 Ti 5:8). You cannot please God by obeying one command (to be a faithful church member) so lavishly that you neglect other equally important rules (such as being a good spouse, parent, employee, and the like).

On the other hand, some people commit the even worse folly of using the list of priorities to excuse an almost total neglect of the church. They have time for everything except the demands of being a valued and dynamic part of a worshipping community.

Happy families sort out these priorities wisely and well, with mutual agreement and support, and with a balanced sense of the Father's will for their household.

## THEY DON'T EXPECT TOO MUCH

Anyone who expects another person to bring happiness will be disappointed – happiness is not something you *get*, but rather something you *give*, and which you then *receive*. Get ready to be let down! No one can fully live up to our expectations of them. Indeed, only when I am myself perfect can I reasonably demand perfection from another.

Nowhere is the need for tolerance more apparent than in the area of sex. This is not the place for a serious study of the matter, but at least let me mention three things –

The *experience* of sex will never equal the *anticipation* of it; it is always better in imagination than in performance! So ignore the text books and the romantic novels – you are not the failure you think you are! [50] Be content to temper your expectations to

---

[50] Never envy the so-called "great lovers" of history and fiction – Casanova, Don Juan, James Bond, and their ilk. Such people, whether male or female, are actually quite pitiful. Full of restless and unrequited hunger, incapable of forming a true and long-lasting liaison with another person, they betray their
. . . . continued on next page.

reality. [51] Much infidelity occurs because people think their spouse has failed them, and that another partner would carry them to the heights of ecstasy they imagine is their due.

It takes years of patient endeavour for a married couple to achieve true congruence, to their fullest mutual fulfilment, common joy,

---

own shallow character. Far from performing prodigies of love, their actions show only that they know nothing at all about it.

[51] Romantic novels often convey an unrealistic hope to their readers. They ascribe to marital love a capacity for rapture that is impossible to achieve. For example, here is a passage adapted from the writings of a popular author –

The pressure of her husband's lips upon hers was not only a rapture and a joy that was indescribable, but was part of everything that was beautiful and inspirational. She felt as if he gave her the light of Olympus and the glitter and the wonder of the gods themselves. There was in his kiss the divine radiance she had sensed in the sweetest poetry, which now seemed to be translated into something real and living. It drew her very soul from between her lips and made it a part of his. His kiss was so perfect, so glorious, that when he raised his head to look down at her, she gave a little murmur as if she could not bear him to let her go, so marvellous was the splendour and ecstasy of their love. . . .

His lips were on hers again and he was kissing her fiercely, passionately, and more insistently than he had before. He felt her quiver against him and now he drew her body closer and closer still  . . . To Lanera it was as if heaven had poured its light upon her so that the sun enveloped her in a golden haze and the glory from it blinded her eyes and swept through her body like a burning flame. Then the light became more intense and the fire of it leaped within them both, carrying them across the starry heavens, merging them with the softly radiant beauty of the moon, and plunging them into the all-consuming heart of the sun. All the beauty of the universe, the fragrance of every rose, the loveliness of the lilies, seemed to coalesce within their enraptured hearts.

As they became one, they found the perfection of love for which everybody yearns. In its purity and beauty their love transformed them. They were no longer human, but divine. They became a part of God, who is perfect beauty and shines as a dazzling light, leading true lovers out of darkness and into an eternal joy.

Charming words! But any man who expects a woman to bring him such supernal happiness, or any woman who expects her man to do so, will inevitably be disappointed. Married love is delightful, but it is not *that* good!

and divine benediction. That is why the idea of a pre-marital "trial" – to see whether a couple is compatible – is so absurd. First love is exciting, and a young wedded couple should certainly enjoy a rapturous and fiery union. But the best pleasures, the sweetest joys, the deepest satisfactions of married love cannot be found until a couple have lived, laughed, wept, worked, and played together for many years.

Don't get too serious about sex. People make love behind locked doors, not because sex is somehow unclean, but because it is private, holy, and most of all (aside from true love) *ridiculous*! So keep a sense of humour. Your partner is not an angel, nor the model for a classic sculpture, but an ordinary person, with a fair share of warts and blemishes. Anyone who seeks perfection in a fellow human will discover only frustration. Happy couples have learned how to laugh at themselves and at each other. They understand not only the heavenly beauty of their union but also its earthy absurdities; they feel not only its divine character but its mundane reality. And they expect nothing more from each other than what two ordinary people can reasonably hope to attain.

## THEY ARE RESOLVED TO LOVE

In scripture, love is not something you feel, but something you do! Whether or not we feel like loving, it remains a command to be obeyed. As the years pass by the fiery aspects of the marital union necessarily fluctuate and eventually abate. But true conjugal love waxes ever deeper and stronger.

A major foundation of such ever-growing love is the recognition that there is an infinite beauty to be discovered in one's spouse. No matter how long two people live together, they will never fully know each other. There are always new depths to descry, and new delights to discover. Each person is a fathomless mystery, and to explore the boundaries of our human enigma would take a hundred lifetimes.

Couples whose love is based, not upon some merely surface attraction, but upon an unshakeable decision to love faithfully until death parts them, can find in each other an inner beauty whose joys are inexhaustible.

Christ is our example, who loved the church (says Paul) when she was deformed, blemished, and rebellious – yet gave himself for her, promising to redeem her by his blood and bring her into his uttermost glory! So should we love each other in Christ.

## POINTS TO PONDER

➤ Examine the level of communication in your own home or family. Do its members disclose too little or too much about themselves? The same question might be asked about the "family" that is the local church.

➤ A pastor commits adultery, but repents, and reverts to righteous behaviour. Ten years later the woman is smitten by guilt, and feels she must tell the world about her fault. She also names the pastor, whose life and ministry are at once ruined. Was she right to include him in her confession?

➤ How much right do you have to tell other people that they have hurt or offended you in some way?

➤ What should you do if you know that you have done some harm, or caused some offence, to another person?

## CHAPTER FIFTEEN:

# YES! AND AMEN!

*We have told you about the Son of God, Christ Jesus, who never wavers between 'yes' and 'no'. With him it is always **'Yes!'** I mean, that on our behalf he is heaven's 'yes' to every promise God has ever given us. But in our turn, when we are praising God, we must say **'Amen!'** to each promise through that same Jesus Christ (2 Co 1:19-20).*

Paul had broken his word! He had promised to visit Corinth while on his way to Macedonia, and then again on his way back (vs. 16). But some troubles in "Asia" (vs. 8) had obliged him to change his plans and now he was unable to come. At once his enemies saw an opportunity to accuse him of being untrustworthy. Even worse, they scorned his *message*, calling it as unreliable as the apostle himself (vs. 17-18).

Paul vigorously defended both his honour and his gospel, and then climaxed his protest by seizing the moment (as he always did) to say something wonderful about Christ –

*No matter how many promises God has made, they are all **'YES'** to us in Christ; but the **'AMEN'** must be spoken by **us**, to the glory of God in Christ.*

How did Christ say **"YES"** to the promises? How must we say **"AMEN"**?

## CHRIST SAYS "YES" TO ALL GOD'S PROMISES

In one of his ballads the Canadian poet Robert Service tells about a neighbour of his in the bohemian quarter of Paris, just before the first World War. The young man was a painter whose entire life's work lay unsold and unwanted in his dingy garret. Yet his passion and his dreams of beauty were no less than those of any other artist, for like them he too had

> . . . burned to throw on canvas everything he saw,
> Twilight on water, tenderness of trees,
> Wet sands at sunset, and the smoking seas,
> The peace of valleys, and the mountain's awe.

But eventually he had to accept the bitter truth that his talent was mediocre. No one else would ever see in his poor daubs the visions that had moved him so deeply. So he resolved to end his life. But first he destroyed every one of his canvasses, and then, in his final moments, raised a wild, despairing lament – [52]

> "Oh, why does God create such men as I? –
> All pride, and passion, and divine desire,
> Raw, quivering nerve-stuff, and devouring fire,
> Foredoomed to failure, though they try and try;
> Unfound, unfit to grapple with the world . . .

In some things we are all like that young man: *"foredoomed to failure, though we try and try!"* – condemned by earlier faults and follies to keep on falling short of the glory of God.

In one place, Paul uses two archery terms to describe our condition.[53] Among Greek bowmen, the first word (*"sinner"*) referred to an arrow that had gone sadly wide of the mark, missing the target altogether. The second (*"fall short"*), described an arrow that had been aimed true, right on the target's centre, but failed to get there. Paul was saying something like this –

---

[52] Ballads of a Bohemian, Book Two, "Early Summer", 'My Neighbours - The Painter Chap'; T. Fisher Unwin, London, 1921; pg. 94.

[53] See Romans 3:23, *"We have all sinned and so keep on falling short of the glory of God."*

*Because in the past we missed the target completely,
now we keep on falling short of it.*

That is, since we have all sinned at some time (shot wide of the target of holiness), we now find, even when our aim is true, that we cannot reach the target. We lack the strength to send an arrow all the way. No matter how hard we try, we cannot get our shaft into the gold.

Every Christian experiences this. We yearn to reach the glory of God in all our words and actions, but sin has so weakened us that even our best endeavours fall short of the mark.

That is why we need Christ to say "YES" to the promises of God on our behalf – not because there is any deficiency in the *promises*, but because *we* are deficient. Indeed, if I look for some reason in myself to believe that the promise is mine, I cannot find it. My sinful nature undermines any claim I might make, mocking any pretensions to righteousness or personal merit before God.

But then I turn to Christ, and hear him say "YES!" to all God's promises on my behalf. How can he do this? By what right? Upon what claim?

Christ is able to make this unquenchable affirmation upon a twofold basis –

> ### *his earthly work of atonement*

Through his voluntary death Christ has secured a pardon for all our sin and a guarantee of eternal life. As scripture says –

> *Christ loved us, and gave his life for us, offering himself as a fragrant sacrifice, well-pleasing to the Father (Ep 5:2).*

> ### *his heavenly work of intercession*

> *Christ is able to save to the uttermost all those who come to God through him, because now he lives forever, interceding for us in heaven (He 7:25).*

So, both *sacrificially* and *sacerdotally* Christ has provided the basis upon which we who trust him may expect all God's promises to be made freely available to us. He is both the Offering and the Offerer, the Priest and the Provision, the Sacrifice and the Saviour, the Guerdon and the Guarantor.

Suppose, for example, that I should begin doubting the promise of bodily healing. I find myself asking, "Does healing belong to me, or not? Can I claim healing of this sickness that has me in its grip, or would such a claim be presumptuous? Should I expect a miracle, or must I simply accept that my disease is the will of God?"

When such questions assail me (whether about healing or any other promise), I need only contemplate Calvary for a few moments. I think about the Saviour's death and resurrection, and I listen to the words he speaks as my Intercessor in heaven.

At once I know that God's answer must be *"YES! YES! YES!"* He cannot deny the finished work of the Cross nor the fervent pleas of his Son! Thus Christ becomes for me the Father's *"YES!"* to every promise he has ever spoken.

Do you think the Father is saying *"No!"* to you? Do you think he is denying you a sweet promise that you know is in the Bible, yet somehow you cannot bring yourself to hope it will happen to you? Turn to Jesus! Look at the Cross! Listen to him interceding for you!

In response to whatever promise the Father has ever spoken to his people, Christ brings an eternal *"YES!"*

The writer of *Hebrews* (2:14-17) sums this up in a remarkable way. He reminds us that there were two groups of fallen creatures in God's universe: a company of angels; and the human race. God decided to redeem just one of those groups; but which one? Surely, says an observer, he will turn to the *angels*? They are much more splendid than those other wretched beings of flesh and blood! Why should God bother with such low creatures? He will certainly prefer to restore the heavenly host to its pristine blazing splendour, radiant and glorious beyond telling! But no, the astonished observer discovers that the Son of God will be born, will die and rise again, and will make everlasting intercession, not for *fallen angels*, but for *fallen people*!

To us, it seems too good to be true! Yet we cannot doubt it! Ask yourself - "Did he clothe himself with the form of an angel?" No, he deliberately took on the form and substance of a *man*! -

> *Jesus wanted to call <u>us</u> (not angels) his children. So since we are people of flesh and blood, he had to become like us, sharing our nature, living the same way we do. He wanted, by his own death, to destroy both the power of death and the one who controlled it, the Devil. Jesus succeeded so well that now he is able to liberate all who were once the slaves of death and to loose us from all our fears (He 2:13-15).*

Nonetheless, no matter how much Christ is God's *"Yes!"* to every promise, those promises will remain unfulfilled unless we express a believing assent to them. Hence Paul adds a second component to the equation -

## WE MUST SAY "AMEN" TO ALL GOD'S PROMISES

I suggest that this means at least three things -

### OPEN YOUR <u>EYES</u> TO SEE THE PROMISE OF GOD

One of the more prevalent faults among western Christians is a poverty of spiritual vision. We are so much engrossed by the surrounding natural world that we have lost the capacity to see clearly into the spiritual dimension. We should instead strive to be like Zecharaiah, who we are told *"<u>lifted</u> up his eyes, and <u>looked</u>, and <u>saw</u>!"* (1:18; 2:1; 5:1; 6:1). Indeed, this capacity to look beyond the veil into the realm of God, to see vividly what is happening in the heavenlies, was a key factor in the invincible faith of all the spiritual heroes described in scripture (cp. He 11:1-39). As Paul said,

> *We Christians have learned how to fix our eyes not on those things that are seen, but rather upon the unseen. We know that the visible world is only temporary, but the invisible one will last for ever! (2 Co 4:18).*

To the eye of faith, the invisible realm of the Spirit is always more real, more substantial, more to be trusted, than the visible natural world. Faith, after all, brings

> *an assurance of the things we still hope for and makes us certain of the things we <u>do not yet see</u> (that is, with the natural eye; (He 11:1),*

– and it was by such faith that the spiritual warriors of old both won their battles and God's approval (vs. 2).

The most important part of this inner or spiritual vision is to realise that behind every promise of God stands a greater reality (whether of pardon, healing, victory, supply, and so on), which the eye of faith can see – and indeed *must* see – if the promise is to be activated (cp. Ep 1:18). That is, behind, say, the promise of physical healing stands a miracle of answered prayer, an image of the sick person made well, the reality of disease defeated and of the promise made good.

We should echo the prayer of Elisha for his young friend, *"Lord, open his eyes so that he may see!"* (2 Kg 6:17). The prophet and all who were with him were about to be captured and killed by the Syrian army - or at least, so it seemed. But Elisha laughed at the peril, crying, *"Those who are fighting for us far outnumber those who are on the enemy's side!"* (vs. 16). He could see what his companions had so far failed to see: the Syrian army was completely surrounded by a vast host of armed angelic warriors, with horses and fiery chariots, who were spread out across the plain, up over the mountains, and on into the heavens, to the very throne of God. The prophet saw the *reality* (an invincible army) that stood behind the *promise* (*"our allies outnumber our foe"*). Without that vision the promise seemed empty. The young man heard it, but was still afraid, until his eyes were opened in response to Elisha's prayer. Then he saw what Elisha could see. Fear at once vanished, faith leaped up to meet the promise, and the miracle was done!

## OPEN YOUR <u>HEART</u> TO BELIEVE
## THE PROMISE OF GOD

We are too often like the disciples whom Jesus rebuked because they were hard of heart and slow to believe (Lu 24:25). How can we break this stony shell? One weapon that smashes unbelief is *prayer*. Notice the example of Daniel –

> *"A revelation came to Daniel . . . The message he received was true; yet only after much struggle was he able to understand the vision as it unfolded before him" (Da 10:1)* -

> ➢ the *revelation* Daniel received is described in vs. 4-9

> ➢ his *struggle* to grasp its meaning, in vs. 2-3

> ➢ the *understanding* that finally came to him, in vs. 10-12.

In the meantime, notice how Daniel's companions ran away from the word of God (vs 7-9), just as many do today, unwilling to contend either with it or for it. Consequently, they miss both *revelation* <u>and</u> *understanding*.

See also *Colossians 1:9-10a*, which shows the need to pray over, and around, and through the word of God, until its spiritual reality has taken possession of your heart, until nothing else seems so tangible as that word, until beside it all else seems insignificant and insubstantial. Faith will then stand secure, rooted in the promise of God, sure of an answer from heaven, rejoicing in the victory it can already see! Where such faith exists there is no room left for despondency, nor can there be any admission of defeat. As the beloved disciple cried, *"This the victory that <u>overcomes</u> the world, even our <u>faith</u>!"* (1 Jn 5:4).[54]

## OPEN YOUR MOUTH TO SPEAK THE PROMISE OF GOD

Every promise of God is certainly ours. They come to us as God's gift in Christ. Nonetheless we are expected to rise up in faith and boldly pronounce an *"AMEN!"* to each of those promises -

> *"On our behalf Christ has indeed said 'Yes!' to all God's promises; but now in Christ we must speak the 'Amen!' to the glory of God."*

*"Speaking the 'Amen!'"* means more than just mouthing one of God's promises, in some ritualistic or formulaic way; and it is much more than merely repeating the two syllables *"a-men"* at the end of a prayer. Notice the strange expression Paul uses: *"THE Amen"*. [55] It is a method in Greek of conveying the idea of a solemn, deliberate, final act of affirmation. There is nothing careless, indifferent, or casual in this *"Amen!"* Rather, it is spoken firmly, boldly, as a confident affirmation and a seal of faith upon the promise.

We can gain an idea of what saying *"<u>the</u> Amen!"* requires from us by asking two questions -

> ➢ How did Jesus say "YES" to the promises of God? *Answer:* - he affirmed the promises to us by a total commitment of himself to the will and word of God, even to the point of death.

---

[54] "Faith" here means two things: it is a synonym for the gospel message, the "faith" of the whole church; and it refers also to each Christian's individual faith.

[55] That is how the Greek text reads; not, *"say Amen,"* but, *"say <u>the</u> amen"*.

➢ How should we say "AMEN" to the promises of God? *Answer:* - by the same quality of total commitment of ourselves, body, soul, and spirit, to the truth and reliability of those same promises.

When Christ says *"YES!"* to the promises of God, and we truly say *"AMEN!"* to them, they sparkle into life! Doubt and despair are banished, and we find ourselves on the path to a marvellous fulfilment of all the good things that lie in the Father's purpose for his children.

With such dazzling secrets now disclosed let us cast aside all unworthy despondency and live joyfully in the radiant life of Christ!

144

## POINTS TO PONDER

➤ Can you agree with the poet that we are all "foredoomed to failure, though we try and try"? If so, what should we do about it? Must we brand ourselves as failures and lapse into pessimism?

➤ How much does a life of victorious faith depend upon a capacity to *"see the invisible"*?

➤ What is the best guarantee you and I have that (in the words of an old gospel song) "every promise in the book is mine, every chapter, every verse, every line"?

➤ Ponder this saying: "Prayer without the Word tends to shallow emotionalism; the Word without prayer tends to arid intellectualism."

➤ How much does a failure to "say THE Amen" contribute toward the scarcity of answered prayer in the modern church?

# BIBLIOGRAPHY

Aesop for Children, The; Rand McNally & Co. Chicago, 1984.

Anglican Prayer Book; 1662.

Ballads of a Bohemian; Robert Service; T. Fisher Unwin, London, 1921

Best Loved Poems of the American People, The; selected by Hazel Felleman; Doubleday; New York 1936.

Canterbury Tales, The; tr. by Nevill Coghill; Penguin Classics, 1977.

Decimus Magnus Ausonius; (310-395) *Epigrams.*

Demonology; Ken Chant; Vision Publishing; Ramona Ca.

Encyclopedia of World Proverbs; Wolfgang Mieder; Prentice-Hall Inc, New Jersey, 1986.

Faith Dynamics; Ken Chant; Vision Publishing; Ramona Ca.

Histories, The; Volume Two; William Shakespeare; The Heritage Press; 1958.

History of the English-Speaking Peoples, The; Winston Churchill; The Folio Society; 2003.

Hymns For Little Children; Cecil Frances Alexander; 1848.

Introduction to Homiletics; Academia Books; Grand Rapids.

Life of Johnson; Boswell;1747.

Montaigne, Selected Essays; tr. Charles Cotton & W. Hazlitt; The Modern Library; Random House Inc. New York, 1949.

Old Testament Commentary; Keil & Delitzsch.

Paradigms Lost; John L. Casti; Cardinal Books; London, 1989.

Pilgrim's Progress; John Bunyan; 1678.

Plays and Poems; Oscar Wilde; ed. Merlin Holland; The Folio Society; London, 1993.

Promoting Change Through Brief Therapy; Gary J. Oliver; Monty Hasz & Matthew Richburg; Tyndale House Publishers; Wheaton Ill. 1997.

Proverbs in Prose; Goethe (1749-1832).

Rebecca and Rowena; W. M. Thackeray.

Recovering From The Losses of Life; H. Norman Wright; Fleming H. Revel; Grand Rapids, Mi. 1993.

Road Less Travelled and Beyond, The; M. Scott Peck; Rider Books; London, 1997.

Silver Poets of the Sixteenth Century; ed. Gerald Bullett; J. M. Dent & Sons Ltd. London, Sirach; The Apochrypha.

Sketches of Moral Philosophy; Sydney Smith (1771-1845),

Strong Reasons; Ken Chant; Vision Publishing; Ramona Ca.

Tennyson's Poetry; ed. Robert W. Hill Jr. W.W. Norton & Co. New York, London, 1971.

Tragedies, The; Volume One & Volume Two; Shakespeare; The Heritage Press; Norwalk Ct. 1958.

Unmasking Male Depression; Archibald D. Hart; Word Publishing; Nashville, 2001.

Why I Am Not A Christian; Lord Bertrand Russell; Unwin Books, London, 1975.